Order a copy of my book and boycott delta airlines

You Would Be PARANOID Too if This Happened To You

U.S. Destructive Practices

Revised 2023

A True Story Told by
Dr. Tyrone Waters, D.D., DRS.
On The Subject of Mental Health

ARPress
45 Dan Road Suite 15
Canton MA 02021

Hotline: 1(888) 821-0229
Fax: 1(508) 545-7580

Ordering Information:
Quantity sales. Special discounts are available on quantity purchases by corporations, associations, and others. For details, contact the publisher at the address above.

Printed in the United States of America.
ISBN-13:   Softcover   979-8-89676-644-5
                eBook   979-8-89676-645-2

Library of Congress Control Number: 2020910353

RIGHTING A WRONG

THE PEOPLE WHO ABUSE THE TRUST

IN GOVERNMENT U.S. DESTRUCTIVE PRACTICES

BY

HOLISTIC LIFE COACH

REV. DR. TYRONE WATERS, D.D., D.R.S., F.H.L.C.A.

WITH

DEEPEST SYMPATHY

Lord, you give grace

to all those in need.

When I feel overwelmed,

help me stand strong.

When I am weary, give me resilience.

When I am sick,

bring me health in

mind and body.

With your help, Lord,

I will serve yyou

to the best of my ability

Amen.

The Portland Observer **Black History Month**   February 29, 2012

Advocating for Disability Rights

In January, Tyrone Waters was honored by Disability Rights Oregon with a plaque to thank him for his six years of volunteer service on its Board of Directors.

As a Board member, Waters helped guide the non-profit organization and support its mission to promote and defend the rights of individuals with disabilities in Oregon.

Waters is the son of former

Tyrone Waters

Oregon State Sen. Avel Gordly. Like his mother, he is a community advocate and volunteers time promoting the rights of all people with a focus on individuals in the mental health system and the African American community.

Waters has released a CD that tells about his encounters with the Portland police and the Oregon State Hospital as an African-American man.

USS RANGER MUSEUM FOUNDATION

Before the board meeting of the USS Ranger Museum Foundation, 40 board members, supporters and guests socialized Jan. 26 at The Monarch Hotel in Clackamas. They were treated to a visit by the board chairman, Retired Navy Vice Admiral Walter Davis of San Diego. The foundation is working to save the aircraft carrier from being sunk as a target, instead bringing it to Portland for use as a museum as well as educational, event and emergency communications centers.

My name is Tyrone Waters. And this is my life story. I was born January 9, 1966 in Portland, Oregon, Multnomah County at Emanuel Hospital weighing just over seven pounds. My father is former U.S. Army Captain Neshelle Waters. My mother, Avel Gordly, is a former Oregon State Senator and Portland State University professor in the Black Studies Department and goes by her maiden name. My childhood was pleasant. I lived with my mother and my grandparents growing up and, occasionally, with my father. My parents were divorced when I was still a baby. And my father died of cancer in 1997 from cigarette smoking, lung cancer to be exact. I went to grade school in the 70's at Irvington Elementary. I went to middle school at Fernwood Middle School and went to high school at Benson Polytechnic High School in the 80's, all in Portland, Oregon where I was raised.

I am a U.S. Navy veteran of the Persian Gulf conflict of the 80's. I served and had the pleasure of being aboard the U.S.S. Ranger with the first African American commanding officer, Captain Walter Davis of an aircraft carrier. I was an aviation structural mechanic in the Navy and worked on airplanes and hydraulic systems on various Naval aircraft. I received a meritorious unit accommodation, a good conduct medal and an honorable discharge. After being discharged from the Navy, I returned to Portland, Oregon where I was harassed by the Portland Police.

On September 23, 1988, on the corner of Southwest 3rd and Taylor in downtown Portland, Officer David Poole and another unnamed Officer stopped me and some friends. I filed a police auditing committee complaint. And it is as follows: Mr. Waters and a friend were stopped by two mounted police officers and asked to show identification. At this time, another friend of Mr. Waters stepped out of Mr. Water's car and was given a pedestrian violation for supposedly stepping off the curb into the street. Mr. Waters alleges that at this time Officer Poole and his partner made sarcastic remarks concerning the viability of these men being gay homosexuals and that they were prostitutes. After filing the complaint with the Portland Police Bureau, Police Chief Richard D. Walker of the Portland Police Bureau wrote the following response on November 10, 1988. "It is unfortunate that you took offense at a line of questioning that informed you that a specific area of town is used by homosexuals to engage in male prostitution. The Officers have a responsibility to interdict criminal activity of that nature whenever possible. Please be assured that we are continually striving to provide the best possible police service, but cannot do so unless we are given an opportunity to look into matters such as the one you brought to our attention. If you should have any questions about the investigation or disposition, please contact Lieutenant Maryanne Hysler of the Internal Investigations Division. This letter will be sent by both regular and certified mail. The notice of enclosure are from the Police Internal Investigation Auditing Committee. And there was a carbon copy sent out to Captain Webber and also Officer Poole. Your rights appeal will be lost unless you comply with the appeal procedures in the enclosure."

After leaving the Navy and returning to Portland and experiencing harassment with the Portland Police Department, I went to work for Delta Airlines as a ramp agent where I experienced intimidation, harassment and racism. What rights does an employee have in this country if he or she is discriminated against or harassed or assaulted on the job? What if the individual kept a daily log of all the incidents that occurred above, including writing a letter to the CEO of the company explaining the incidents that occurred and nothing is done about it? What if the individual who complains about such unfair practice reports the problem to them and the supervisor and then is blamed or accused of causing the problem, when in actuality the company chooses to blame the victim and fire the victim? Not only did this happen to me, but Delta Airlines Incorporated has a history of these practices in the Portland, Oregon station. One man, a station operations manager, and supervisors and co-workers caused all of these incidents to happen and more.

When I reported these incidents to the Civil Rights Division of Oregon and filed a complaint with EEOC and the federal government, they claimed that there was no evidence. But how do you explain being called "Nigger." And how do you explain being pushed and punched? How do you explain police reports? How do you explain reporting twenty-five incidents to supervisors and nothing being done about it? What type of an airline is Delta Airlines if it allows such practices to go on in the workplace and then fired the victim for complaining about such practices? Is this the type of airline that you would want to fly, or for that matter, the type of airline that you would want your family to fly? If all these things go on around an aircraft prior to it's departure, imagine the safety checks that are being overlooked and neglected due to the ignorance of a bunch of people who have racist ideas about who they believe should work in their all-White, male dominated occupation?

The reason for writing this is to shed light on the real life horror story that occurred at Delta Airlines in Portland, Oregon at Portland International Airport back in 1988. When you finish hearing this, it will make you say how could such a thing happen and not one person stand up and help the victim? It's easy. Racism is still alive in the airline industry and nothing is being done to bring about change. You see, not all people are violent or react in a violent way to racism. But if you report it on the job and then an investigation is preformed and names are asked for by the supervisor and the manager of the co-employees that are harassing me, then the supervisors do nothing about it. And the co-workers are allowed to retaliate against me. And nothing is done about that. How do you explain that? All of the supervisors were aware of what was going on. But yet, the station manager in Portland, Oregon said that he was unaware. What kind of man could be in charge of such a station at Portland, and be unaware of a problem that existed in one of his departments? And why did all of the supervisors working in the department fail to let the station manager know what was going on?

When I was asked to give the names of the individuals who were giving me a hard time on the job, all the company would have done was find a way to blame the victim. I was the one working in a hostile environment with these people. I was not the destructive element in the workforce. They did a lot of disruptive things to me. And the individuals who caused all of this madness were not held accountable. The Delta Airline solution to all of this was to fire and blame the victim.

On May 7, 1990, I wrote a letter to the Chairman of the Board and Chief Executive Officer of Delta Airlines. And it reads as follows: "Sir, I would like to bring to your attention some concerns of mine regarding working conditions in Department 120 at Portland International Airport. These are very serious concerns. And this needs to be brought to your attention before I take further action. I am sending this for you records. During the past several months, I have experienced problems on the job. I have been pushed physically by several co-workers. I've had passenger bags thrown directly on me in the aircraft bin, in an unsafe manner. I've had my locker broken into and items stolen out of it and hate mail put into my mailbox. I have been called racial and sexual obscenities, which I consider to be offensive. I am the only Black person on my shift. My co-workers and management staff are making conditions unbearable so that I cannot function. And I am beginning to feel stressed. And I feel that they are conspiring against me to fire me from my job, as well as cause bodily harm to me. I have complained about the harassment. Again, I am bringing this to your attention because I know you are not aware of this. I anxiously look forward to your response. Respectfully, Tyrone Waters."

On August 24, 1990, I received a letter from the Federal Aviation Administration, Flight Standards District Office, Federal Aviation Administration, Portland, Oregon. "Dear Mr. Waters, Our office received a letter from the Oregon Occupational Safety and Health Division regarding several safety hazards alleged by you on Delta Airlines. Subsequent inspections have been accomplished by this office to verify these allegations. During these inspections some of the safety issues mentioned in your report were verified by our safety inspectors. We are now taking action to insure that these issues are corrected and have scheduled further inspections to verify continued compliance with the federal aviation regulations and safe operating practices. We would like to thank you for bringing this to our attention. If we can be of further assistance, please give us a call. Sincerely, Aviation Safety Inspector Richards."

On April 4, 1990, I filed a Civil Rights complaint with the Bureau of Labor and Industries Civil Rights Division. They responded by saying, "If your complaint falls under the jurisdiction of Federal Civil Rights laws, we will file a complaint with the Federal authorities unless you ask us not to. The sooner we receive your completed questionnaire, the sooner we can act on it. Please remember to compete all blanks, giving dates and names and addresses of witnesses. Sincerely, Civil Rights Division."

I filed a federal lawsuit in Federal U.S. District Court against Delta Airlines with me being the plaintiff, Tyrone Waters. U.S. Magistrate Jelderks wrote, "In an order dated March 20, 1992, the Court ordered that a pretrial order be lodged by June 1, 1992. No pretrial order was lodged. In an order dated June 30, 1992, the Court ordered that the parties appear in writing by July 10, 1992 to show cause why this case should not be dismissed for want of prosecution. Defendant had filed a response setting out the chronology of extensions of deadlines for completing discovery, filing motions and lodging of the pretrial order which has been granted at Plaintiff's request. Plaintiff has not responded to the order to show cause. And this action should be dismissed for want of prosecution. Dated the 16th day of July, 1992. John Jelderks, United States Magistrate Judge."

While things were proceeding with the Delta Airlines case, I had been harassed by the Portland Police again. And I was stopped and cited on 1-28-92 at 1:30 p.m. and given an offense of careless driving. Also on that day, at the same time, I was given offense of attempt to allude a police officer and arrested and taken into custody. The very next day, I had depositions at Delta Airlines attorney's office here in Portland, Oregon. And the first question that came out of their mouths was what did I do the night before? Fortunately, I was released from custody so that I could go to the deposition. But clearly, you can see what efforts were used to try to discredit me.

Also, while the Delta case was going on, I was hospitalized at both Emanuel Hospital in Portland, Oregon and Portland Adventist Hospital for stress and exhaustion. After being released from both hospitals for stress and exhaustion, and finding out that the case was dismissed for want of prosecution, I tried to find another job. I went from job to job to job, endlessly losing one job after another. And this went on for years.

My name is Tyrone Waters. And this is my story. I have a mental illness. I was first diagnosed with paranoid schizophrenia in 1995. It has been a long battle and struggle for me to manage the constraints of my illness. It is a day to day struggle. But most recently, for the past several years the disease schizophrenia has been easier to deal and cope with, namely because of a newly prescribed medication which is called Risperdal, four milligrams taken once a day at bedtime. Bedtime for me is at 7:00

p.m. each night. It has also been easier to deal and cope with the illness by having tremendous support from friends and family and my higher power. I mentioned bedtime as being 7:00 p.m., seven nights as week. And it is due to a side-effect of my medication, which makes me drowsy and tired. But I'm still able to function. The best way to describe how it feels is it's like you're fighting to stay awake on the medication. But this medication, Risperdal, provides quality of life which I otherwise would not have.

I was pretty much jobless, with an occasional temporary job here and there. Life became stressful. I began thinking paranoid thoughts. I began thinking people were out to get me and that they were following me. I felt the walls of my world closing in around me slowly, as though I was trapped in a cell with nowhere to go. I became fearful of food and eating out at restaurants, thinking that the employees at the restaurants were doing something to the food. When in all actuality and reality, they had not done anything wrong to the food. But it was my paranoia setting in.

Then in 1995, I had my first serious run-in with the law. I was arrested and accused of attempted arson against a State of Oregon Correctional Officer in her van. She accused me of trying to ignite her van on fire. I did no such thing. The police found a gas can containing water in it in my vehicle at the time of my arrest. I was taken to the Justice Center and booked and charged with attempted arson. It all seemed unreal. Why was this happening to me?

The police strip searched me, took away all of my clothes and gave me a paper suit to wear. I was in jail for ninety days before my attorney decided that I was unable to aid and assist in my own defense, not fit to pursue a trial. So I was ordered by Judge Dorothy Baker to go to the Oregon State Hospital for an evaluation, or until fit to stand trial. I was at the Oregon State Hospital for an additional ninety days before doctors determined and diagnosed me with having a mental illness, schizophrenia.

It has become very clear to me that the State doctors did not know what medication would be appropriate for me. Thus, I had and was forced against my will to try several different medications, some of which were Thorazine, Prolixin, Haldol, Zyprexa and now Risperdal. The State doctors told me that I had a mental illness and that f would need to take medication life-long. I was finally discharged from the State Hospital fit to stand trial. And I took a plea bargain to attempted arson, on the advice of the Public Defender. And I was given five years probation.

I was ordered by Judge Dorothy Baker to stay on my medication, which was Thorazine at the time, and be compliant with the conditions of my probation. After that I met a psychiatrist, Dr. Charles Belville, who had become my psychiatrist. He took me off Thorazine and put me on Zyprexa. I took Zyprexa, on and off for a number of years. And each time I went off my medication, I would wind up in the hospital in a psychiatric unit at the hospital. Zyprexa was not working well for me. I experienced heavy weight gain and found out that Zyprexa can cause diabetes in African Americans. If they continue with the medication they would have weight gain. So I would leave the hospital being put back on Zyprexa, and then a short time after going off of it again.

My next episode or run-in with the law came September 17, 2001. The police had been dispatched to my residence. And when they pulled up, I stepped off a neighbor's porch with a pellet gun in my hand. The police immediately drew their weapons and pointed them at me and told me to drop the gun. At that point, they repeated several times, "Drop the gun." And a swarm or police had arrived on the scene. I had not been taking my medication and my symptoms were severe. I was confused and fearful. I feared that if I flinched or moved or did drop the gun that the police would surely kill me. So I stood still and rigid, not moving, with the gun in my hand. And the police then fired bean bag rounds, three, and two live rounds of ammunition at me. I was struck by the bean bag rounds in my right knee, right buttocks and left wrist. Though the Grace of God, the live rounds missed me. ! fell to the ground. The rest became a blur.

I remember waking up in a lot of pain at Legacy Emanuel Hospital in the emergency room, where my Mother stood by my side of my hospital bed. Several tests were performed, x-ray, blood draw, MRI, etcetera. Then I was strapped to a bed with four-point restraints and locked in a room with a police officer standing outside my door. The next morning the police came in my room, handcuffed me and arrested me and took me downtown for booking at the Multnomah County Justice Center jail. This would turn out to be a horrific nightmare for the coming year.

I was ordered by Judge Julie Frantz to get an evaluation at the State Hospital, while still in custody. I had been charged with attempted aggravated murder against one of the police officers from the day of the incident. This man was Portland Police Officer Derrick Foxworth. He was also the Chief of Police at that time. I was found unable to aid and assist, not fit for trial. I still had injuries from being shot. So I went south to Salem, Oregon, in custody, to the Oregon State Hospital for an evaluation and treatment. While at the State Hospital, I was a victim of sexual assault and mistreatment by another patient and by several staff.

My Oregon Health Plan benefits have been cut due to State budget cuts. And I'm now forced to pay for my medications and mental health treatment. I have been hospitalized on psychiatric units both at the State Hospital and private hospitals a total of eight times. Some of us have struggled for many years with our psychiatric illness, while others have just begun to experience the onset of symptoms. Some of us have experienced changes in our ability to perceive reality clearly and have experienced hallucinations. Whether they come in the form of hearing voices or seeing visions, some of us have felt increased energy or have experienced changes in our ability to think and make judgments. We may have found that our thoughts sometimes race and seem to go out of control. Some of us have felt a loss of energy, a loss of enjoyment of life and have perceived life from a negative perspective. Perhaps our sleeping patterns and appetite have changed as well. We may have become suicidal. We may find that we have difficulty with our thoughts and concentration. These lists are far from complete. But they point to a common bond. Both men and women are affected by different types of no-fault illnesses, who's symptoms can disrupt the ability to function and relate to others effectively.

Some of us feared that we were becoming hopelessly impaired. We came to believe that we would never be normal again. Many of us have experienced great shame and guilt. We believe that our emotional or psychiatric illness were our fault. Some of us have become secretive. And later, some of us felt a need to keep our recovery and steps a secret. We also felt our psychiatric illness must be kept secret, especially if our recovery program included prescription medication. We seem to run out of ways to protect our feelings and self-esteem and to protect ourselves from the attitudes of those around us. If there are any among us who have felt as though they were living in that closet, I welcome you. I want you to know that the fear, isolation and secrecy no longer need be a part of your life.

I am Tyrone Waters and this is my story. Here's a little bit about my educational background. I am a graduate of Portland Community College Office Information Systems Program. I am also a graduate of the formerly International Correspondence School, where I completed the Master course in travel. I am also a graduate of Stratford Career Institutes Culinary Le Cordon Bleu Program. I graduated from the Hypnosis Motivation Institute, where I received my certified hypnotist certification. I am also a graduate of the United Bartender's Institute and have my bar tending credentials.

Also, after being in custody and released back into the community, I graduated from the University of Metaphysics in 2004 and received my life coaching credentials and am presently a member in good standing with the Federation of Holistic Life Coaches Association.

I have worked for Cascadia BehavioraJ Healthcare as a mental health peer counselor and have that job just six months after being released from custody and worked for them for several years. I am also on the Board of Directors at Disability Rights Oregon. And I'm also a member and an advisor to the Multnomah County Quality Management Committee. Both Board positions deal with mental health concerns of the mentally ill. And as such, I advocate for the mentally ill that are locked up in prisons, psychiatric units, jails and hospitals.

I have worked at Cascadia Behavioral Healthcare. And while working there, I have experienced sexual discrimination, racism; not from other staff but from other clients. I believe we all can do more to let clients and staff know that racism will not be tolerated. And it is through the continued ignorance of others that it continues to exist. As an employee and a client of Cascadia, I experienced life at Cascadia from both perspectives, as a staff and as a client. And as such1 I educate people on the negative aspects and outcomes of racism in an environment that already has outbursts of hostility due to mental illness. I have, however, had positive experiences dealing with case managers and prescribers as a client, which has helped me in my continued wellness.

My most recent positions with Cascadia Healthcare was back in 2003 through 2007. In 2003, I was a peer advocate counselor. And I counseled and advocated for clients, assisted clients with daily activities, completed charting notes on clients and facilitated community meetings. In 2006, I became a recovery support specialist for Cascadia Behavioral Healthcare and assisted clients to acclimate to the community, provided resources relating to education, housing and employment. I also provided support to enhance client mental health recovery and stability. I also worked with a caseload of more than two hundred clients.

In 2006 through 2007, I worked as a chef, dietary aide, ala carte server with Irvington Village Assisted Living Retirement Community in Portland, Oregon. I prepared resident meals, special orders and desserts, served and distributed resident meals and ala carte entrees. Skilled in providing nutritious food, following restricted diet menus.

And then in 2007, I went back to Cascadia Behavioral Healthcare with their Wellsprings Division and worked as a job skills trainer and life coach. In that capacity, I supervised clients in real life employment situations, helped clients to develop and apply job skills, helped clients in assessing and coordinating care for themselves and monitored symptoms and medication management. I also provided counseling and completed daily progress notes.

In March 2008, the attorney that represented me in my criminal proceedings wrote the following letter of recommendation on March 26, 2008. And it reads as follows: "Letter of recommendation for Tyrone Waters. To whom it may concern: This is a letter of recommendation for my former client, Tyrone Waters. I represented Mr. Waters about seven years ago on Ballot Measure 11 charges in Multnomah County. At the time of the incident that led to Tyrone's indictment, he was suffering from a psychotic delusion caused by schizophrenia. During the course of my representation, he was successfully treated for schizophrenia by a psychiatrist, put on psychotropic medications and successfully addressed his symptoms. Subsequently, over the last seven years I have still been in touch with Mr. Waters. My opinion of him is that he is a man of considerable social skill and integrity. He is one of my few success stories as a criminal defense attorney. And I recommend him for any position for which he may apply. If you would like to discuss Mr. Waters with me, please feel free to contact me. Sincerely, Randall Vogt, Attorney at Law."

In March 2007, I testified to the 2007 Human Services of the Subcommittee of the Ways and Means Committee. Here is that short testimony from Tyrone Waters. "Madame Chair, Members of the Committee, my name is Tyrone Waters and I am a consumer advocate of the mental health system. As well, I serve as a Board member of the Board of Directors at Oregon Advocacy Center. I'd like to say that I was a patient at the Oregon State Hospital. And as such, I experienced horrific treatment and abuse by staff and by another patient who was sent to the State Hospital from the Oregon Department of Corrections Prison System. I was physically assaulted on Ward 48B by a male staff person, Shawn Taylor, and filed an Oregon State police report. I received injuries to my legs .. As well, I also filed a grievance with the State Hospital. I was also physically and sexually assaulted by Oregon State Hospital patient and department corrections inmate, Richard Dickey. I was refused medical care in both incidents. And staff covered it up. My mail was also withheld and my phone privileges were taken away. These are a few incidents that occurred, as well as racial overtones while I was at the State Hospital. There were staff, however, there that were helpful to me while staying there.

But let us not forget people like my dear friend Corey Dennison, a patient that was sexually assaulted by a male hospital staff and filed a grievance that was covered up by hospital staff. Most recently, there was another set of incidents involving patient Corey Dennison, who was physically assaulted on Ward SOF and received twenty-eight stitches after having been assaulted in his eye by another patient, and then transferred to Ward 48C where staff are not allowing him to file a police report with the State Police, and not responding to his filed grievances with the hospital and denying him the right to petition the courts for habeas corpus petition and a writ of mandamus or injunctive relief against the State Hospital.

Over three weeks ago, Corey mailed correspondence addressed to myself and a separate letter mailed to Oregon State Senator Avel Gordly, my mother, none of which have been received. It is apparent that staff are withholding his mail. Shame on the Legislature for allowing the sign to be displayed in front of the State Hospital that reads "People helping People.."When it should say people hindering people.

It is my recommendation to this Legislative body to implement immediately community-based programs for conditional release and placement of patients into the community from the State Hospital forensics program and wards. Let's stop the stalling on this issue.

And I ask furthermore that the legislature order the Superintendant at the State Hospital and his subordinates to improve, increase and implement multicultural diversity and awareness programs for patients and staff, and not a program that is just talked about by hospital officials to this legislative body, but one that is a reality and real model that we can see working in the system.

Madame Chair, Members of the Committee, I did not sue the State of Oregon for the horrific treatment and abuse and atrocities that it caused me. But I am here before you today, and on behalf of patient Corey Dennison, to speak out against it. I swear under oath, that my stated testimony is true and accurate to the best of my ability. Thank you for your time. And I sincerely hope you will give attention to these mentioned issues. Very respectfully submitted this 19th day of March, 2007. Sincerely, Tyrone Waters."

I am continuing my education. And, I am presently enrolled with the Stratford Career Institute Natural Health Consulting Program. Since I have been out of the hospital, and before I went into the hospital, I have had my vehicles tampered with and my apartments and residences tampered with and items stolen out of both my vehicle and my apartments. I have also come home to find my medications tampered with and not the way I left them when I left the apartment and returned. I have also been threatened by my neighbor, who has made racial slurs and has made death threats. I have filed complaints with the Community Development Management that runs my apartment dwelling. And they have done nothing about it. I have filed several police reports against my neighbor for his intimidating behavior and harassment.

I recently lost my job at Cascadia Behavioral Healthcare because the Oregon State Department of Human Services said that I am not allowed to work in an unsupervised position. I had to fife an appeal with regard to that decision. And it was upheld. And I am not allowed to work in an unsupervised position with Cascadia. So I lost my job and am not longer employed with them. It just goes to show how destructive the State government can be and the evils that are out there that exist and that it continues.

Here is a letter written to S. Renee Mitchell, a news reporter at the Portland Oregonian news paper. I wrote this letter to her quite some time ago. And since then, she has left The Oregonian and is no longer employed there. It reads as follows: "Dear Renee, per our conversation today by phone, there are a handful of tenants here, at the Dawson Park Apartments, who are on disability and have a mental illness. Our apartments have been entered without our permission and items removed or tampered with. We have filed police reports to no avail. The harassment continues. We have met with the manager of the building and her superior, as well as owners of the Dawson Park Building. We were also represented by an attorney from Disability Rights Oregon who mediated the meeting. We met with them several weeks ago and nothing was resolved. And again, the harassment continues. I find it very odd and peculiar that four individuals, all receiving disability for mental illness with different diagnoses are being harassed. We would like for this to stop. We ask for your help in publishing a story in The Oregonian about this ongoing harassment. Why is this happening to us? We have the right to live free of harassment and with dignity and respect. Please feel free to contact us to do a story about this horrifying harassment. We have had our food tampered with, our medications tampered with and items moved and stolen from our apartments. Thank you for your time. We all look forward to reading about this in The Oregonian. Sincerely, Tyrone Waters."

The residence that I have lived at over the years from 9-22-83 all the way to 1-6-09 and present are as follows: 5235 N. Minnesota Avenue, 901 SW King Avenue, Apartment 2, 1915 N.E. 16th Avenue, 4511 N. Williams Avenue, 5700 N. Kirby Avenue, Apartment 202, 1510 N.E. Hancock Street, 2525 N. Williams Avenue, Apartment 2, 4511 N. Williams Avenue, 2600 Center Street, Salem, Oregon, 9268 S.E. Clinton Street Apartment 3, 4511 N. Williams Avenue} 101 N. Morris Street, Apartment 315, 1725 S.E. Morrison Street, Apartment 2. I have lived at each and every one of these residences. And at each and every one of these residences my apartment has been gone into, items have been tampered with, stolen and disrupted.

I have had the following vehicles tampered with and items stolen out of the vehicles: 1972 Cadillac Fleetwood sedan, four-dour limousine, license plate number QAY464, 1989 Ford Probe sedan, two-door, license plate number QEA389, 1989 Honda Prelude sedan, two-door, license plate number PWL440. This vehicle was also owned by my Aunt, Faye Burch, who she purchased it for herself several year ago and then gave it to me. Also, 2004 Chevy Impala sedan, four-door, license plate number CKL7427.

Also the following police activity has been reported at my residence at the following dates: Neighbor disturbance problem, 1-5-09 at 1725 S.E. Morrison. 1-16-09, 1725 S. E. Morrison, suspicious activity. 5-27-09, assistance rendered public at 1725 S.E. Morrison. 9-17-09, 1725 S.E. Morrison, threats and intimidation. And prior to that at 101 N. Morris Street on 12-23-07, there was suspicious activity. And prior to that on 10-16-07 at 101 N. Morris Street, there was burglary, resident forced entry.

Here are some names of people with mental illness that enrich our lives, and that have enriched our lives: Abraham Lincoln, Virginia Woolf, Lionel Aldridge, Eugene O'Neill, Beethoven, Gaetano

Donizetti, Jujinski, John Keats, Tennessee Williams, Vincent Van Gogh, Isaac Newton, Ernest Hemingway, Sylvia Plath, Michelangelo, Winston Churchill, Vivien Leigh, Emperor Norton the 1 s t, Jimmy Piersall, Patty Duke, Charles Dickens, Garth Brooks, Mike Tyson, Hans Christian Andersen, Irving Berlin, Art Buchwald, Dick Cavett, Winston Churchill, Dick Clark, Emily Dickinson, Isaac Densen, Jules Pfeiffer, T. S. Elliot, Victor Hugo, Francis Lear, Georgia O'Keefe, Edgar Allan Poe, Jackson Pollock, Cole Porter, Joan Rivers, Mary Shelley, Rod Steiger, William Styron, Mark Twain, Mike Wallace, Walt Whitman,

Bert Yancey, Carrie Fisher, Ted Turner, Alma Powell, Kitty Dukakis, former Oregon State Senator and Portland State University Professor Avel Gordly, Tyrone Waters. These are all people with mental illness that enrich our lives.

I have also been giving educational speeches on mental illness to Doctor/ professor Joy DeGruy's class in the Department of Social Work at Portland State University and the effects of racism and institutionalized systems in mental healthcare, and the impact her students will have in the future when they work in the field.

My mother, former Oregon State Senator Avel Gordly, has championed mental health issues in the State Senate in Oregon and called for the U.S. Department of Justice to investigate the mistreatment and abuses at the Oregon State Hospital. We have not been able to see any positive corrective action, other than the fact that I and other patients were mistreated and abused there. I have continued to monitor conditions at the Oregon State Hospital and report any ongoing progress of the treatment of the patients, as well as abuse, to the proper venues and entities. Although I was raised Catholic as a child, I attend Highland Christian Center in Portland, Oregon for religious services. But I still keep my Catholic faith. I'm Tyrone Waters. I'm a survivor. And this is my life story.

I would like to thank my family and friends for their love and support; my father Neshelle Waters, my mother Avel Gordly, my aunt Faye Burch, my cousin Michelle Burch, my uncle Michael Burch, my uncle

Tyrone Gordly, my Aunt Dean Gordly of Spanaway, Washington, my friend Greg Mackie and the rest of my family and friends, too many to mention. Thank you.

And now, here's some additional information on schizophrenia and expanding the possibilities of how schizophrenia is treated. While there is no cure for schizophrenia yet, research has led to a newer generation of medicines that give new hope. These medicines can help your loved ones manage their symptoms. Medicines for schizophrenia are called antipsychotic drugs. Although the exact way these medicines work is unknown, anti-psychotics are thought to restore the balance of chemicals in the brain so messages don't get confused. Older generation conventional antipsychotic drugs have been around for over fifty years. These drugs manage the positive symptoms of schizophrenia. Newer generation, atypical anti-psychotics have been available for the last fifteen years. These drugs are described as atypical because they are different from conventional anti-psychotics. Atypical anti-psychotics treat both the positive and negative symptoms of schizophrenia.

And now let's talk about understanding schizophrenia. What is schizophrenia? Schizophrenia is a brain disorder that causes people to sometimes have difficulty functioning in their daily lives. Research suggests that schizophrenia may be caused by a chemical imbalance in the brain. This imbalance can produce too many messages which can get mixed up and cause symptoms. Who gets schizophrenia? It is still unknown why this illness happens to one person and not to another. Schizophrenia occurs equally in men and women. Symptoms usually first appear sometime between the young adult years and the early thirties. Only a doctor can accurately diagnose schizophrenia.

What are the symptoms of schizophrenia? People with schizophrenia may experience different types of symptoms. The most common types are positive and negative symptoms. Positive describes an excess of symptoms that are not normally present. Negative describes a lack of behaviors or feelings that are normally present. Positive symptoms include the following: Believing things that most other people do not think are real or true, seeing or hearing things that others do not, feeling very scared and distrustful, taking action without really thinking, and disorganized thoughts. Negative symptoms include the following: Having little or inappropriate feelings in certain situations, feeling disconnected or out of touch with friends and family, having a difficult time speaking with others, and finally, losing interest in regular, every day activities. Ideally, a medication should treat both types of symptoms. If you need help, or assistance or require additional information on schizophrenia or any other mental illness, please contact a mental healthcare professional in your area.

The following is a grievance that I filed on 11-6-2009. "I want to report patient abuse that occurred on 11-5-09 at Kaiser Permanente Medical Facility. I had pain in my lower back and called the advice nurse. She argued about the diagnosis. The nurse recommended an appointment with the provider. I went to the urgency care instead to seek treatment. There, comments were made. 'Your socks stink' 'We want you dead' 'We got Waters' 'We got Gordly, Waters mother's Maiden name' 'You're crazy' On the security guard's radio it was announced, "We got Waters." The check-in receptionist came to his room and started laughing and walked away. I had to leave the facility and had to go to Providence Emergency to be treated. It was very upsetting. I called Medicare to report this abuse.

I also wrote a letter to the United States Department of Justice about the incident on November 7, 2009. And it reads as follows: "Dear Liaison, please be advised that I am enclosing a copy of a grievance dated 11-6- 09 for patient abuse that occurred on 11-5-09 at a Kaiser Permanente facility in Portland, Oregon. I would appreciate your investigating this matter and rendering a response in a timely manner that is expeditious. I have contacted Medicare and also the Office of OIC and was not able to get a resolution to the problem. I also contacted the Governor's ombudsman through Medicare by phone and got no response. Sincerely, Tyrone Waters.."I have not gotten a response from the U.S. Justice Department.

[End of Volume 1]

[Volume 2]

Welcome to volume two of You Would Be Paranoid Too If This Happened To You. I'm Tyrone Waters. I'm going to tell you about the chiropractic doctor, Billy Flowers, who's office address is 2124 N.E. Hancock Portland, Oregon 97212. And his office phone number is 503-287-5504. And, the connection that he had with Delta Airlines when I filed my case against Delta Airlines.

My Mom and I were in an automobile accident. We went to be treated for injuries by Dr. Billy Flowers. While I continued to receive treatment, there was a Delta Airlines employee that would be at all of my doctor's appointments, just outside of Dr. Billy Flower's doctor's office making threats towards me. How did this person know when my appointments were? It's clear that Dr. Flowers was releasing this information to the Delta employee. When I confronted Dr. Flowers about it, he had me arrested for stalking, criminal mischief and criminal trespassing. And I spent thirty days in jail. Is this the kind of doctor you want treating you? Dr. Flowers contracts with Kaiser Permanente. I will never seek medical treatment from Dr. Billy Flowers ever again.

Also when I was homeless and living in a motel room on North Interstate in Portland, Dr. Billy Flowers called my motel room and stated, 'I thought you were dead'. He also stalked me to a motel room in the Seattle area.

And now let me bring up to date on the most recent developments at my apartment at 1725 S.E. Morrison, #2. On 3-27-2010, three cans of black-eyed peas were stolen from my apartment. On 3-28-2010, medications were tampered with in my apartment. On 3-30-2010, the bottom lock was found unlocked and tampered with in my apartment while I was at home. On 4-1-2010, drugs were found on the kitchen counter in my apartment. On 4-2-2010, a notepad of my diary was stolen from my apartment. On 4-9-2010, a work ink pen was missing from my apartment. On 4-14-2010, Qwest telephone company, directly across the street from my apartment building was doing sewer work across the street. On 4-15-2010, Qwest telephone company sealed up the sidewalk across the street in front of their door with cement. On 5-13-2010, an Ibuprofen prescription was stolen from my apartment.

On 5-15-2010, approximately 12:00 noon, James gave me a piece of my mail, a phone bill, and it had been opened. James is my neighbor. On 5-16-2010, James's friend came over at approximately 4:00 p.m. Later in the evening, my friend stopped by. I stepped out of the apartment and closed my door and locked both locks and went down to the curb to talk to my friends. When I returned to my apartment five minutes later, I found the door had been opened and I found the locks unlocked, shortly after 6:00 p.m. There was no one else around except for James in his apartment.

On 5-17-2010, I turned in a copy of my diary to REACH manager Carrie Lewis. She said she would talk to her supervisor about it. This was shortly after 8:30 a.m. They have done nothing about it. On 5-25-2010, I received a letter from REACH, which I will read momentarily. On 6-16-2010, my neighbor James's friend was outside of my backdoor at 3:52 a.m. trying to get in. I banged on the door from the inside of my apartment and his friend ran off the back porch over to James's apartment. And I heard James yell out loud to his friend and say, "You blew it.,, On 6-22-2010, I left my apartment at approximately 10:00 a.m. and returned at 1:00 p.m., approximately. And when I entered my apartment, I found three pen marks on my recliner chair that were not there when I left at 10:00 a.m. I called police to file a report. And I called REACH to report vandalism. REACH said they could not hear me on the phone.

In a letter dated May 25, 2010 from REACH it reads as follows: "Regarding your note received May 20th and telephone call on May 18th. Dear Mr. Waters, I have reviewed your list of concerns and allegations about your neighbor Mr. Stovell, as well as the previous concerns you have raised, the police reports we have received and other correspondence. I have also reviewed all notices and actions taken by REACH with Mr. Stovell. As you know privacy restrictions prevent me from releasing any information about one resident to another resident. However, I can assure you that each incident has been followed up and appropriate actions have been taken. REACH has responded to each of your previous concerns. And your lock has been changed a number of times. If you have additional third-party confirmation of your allegations about missing items; canned foods, pen, notebook, over the counter medicine, etcetera, lock tampering or the appearance of drugs, I would welcome that information. If you wish to consider moving to a different property managed by REACH, I would encourage you to review our property listings on the REACH website. You may want to request assistance from Austin Irvman to identify those properties you may be interested in and complete waiting list applications. Or if you feel that Austin's assistance in trying to resolve differences with your neighbor would be beneficial, I would encourage you to talk with him. Since you are unhappy with REACH, you may want to consider moving to a property owned and managed by some other group. Sincerely, Margaret M. Mahoney, Director of the Property Management"

Before I moved to this apartment, I lived in the Dawson Park Apartments. And I lived in apartment 315 in Portland, Oregon. The apartment directly above mine, they would play subliminal messages day and night. When I moved to 1725 S.E. Morrison #2, the apartment above me, #6, also has been playing subliminal messages, day and night since day one when I first moved in. The Manager, Tracy Darwin, at the Dawson Park Apartments, asked REACH where I was moving to. And they disclosed that information to her. Also, approximately a year ago there was a death of an African American male in apartment #6. The coroner and police were called to the scene. I am now the only African American male living in this housing complex.

On May 5, 2010, Kaiser Permanente sent me the following correspondence, responding to a complaint that I had filed: "Dear Mr. Waters, We were notified by the Center for Medicare and Medicaid Services about a complaint you filed. Your concern regarded services you received on November 5, 2009 in the Urgent Care Department on the Interstate Medical Office Campus. This letter is in response to your complaint, which Medicare defines as a grievance. Thank you for taking the time to share your serious concerns with us. It is important that we hear from our members who are unhappy with the service they receive. Mr. Waters, for your convenience I have enclosed a copy of the letter sent to you on November 25, 2009. This letter addresses your complaint about the service you received in the urgent care department on November 5th. As documented in the letter, your concerns were shared with managers in the urgent care and medical advice departments, where we review and follow-up with involved staff as appropriate. Mr. Waters, we apologize for any frustration and worry you may have experienced about the service you received in the urgent care department in November of 2009.

I hope this fetter provides you reassurance that your concern has been taken very seriously and thoroughly investigated. We are committed to providing the highest quality care to our members. We sincerely appreciate being made aware of those situations where we have fallen short of our members' expectations. We have an internal review process for researching patient concerns about quality of care and any actions with Kaiser Permanente providers. Your concerns have been documented and forwarded on for this quality review. The results are confidential. However, please be assured your concerns will receive careful consideration and appropriate follow-up. We also want you to know that you have a right to pursue an independent review of your care concerns. If you are concerned about the quality of care you received, including care during hospital stay, you can also complain to an independent quality review organization called the QYA."

United States Statute 18 USD, Section 9231 reads as follows: "The listener could be placed in fear, harm or death. And what is the intent an objectionable, reasonable listener would have when placed in fear or death by ways or means of a subliminal message. And that message should be barred by inter-state commerce."

On June 29, 2010, I wrote the following letter to the Oregon State Bar Disciplinary Section in Tigard, Oregon: "To the Oregon State Bar. As a person who had to await trial and then settle for a plea bargain, it is unfair, inhumane, brutal, vexatious and redundant behaviors that I was subjected to. Also, by placing me under duress to force a plea bargain is illegal in this State. In this State, suicide is the eighth leading cause of death, third among youth. Do you know why? These are the abusive powers used by District Attorney Mike Schrunk, the Multnomah

County Sheriff, the Portland Police Chief, the Portland Mayor, the Portland City Attorney and the Multnomah County Commissioners, as well as the Governor and Attorney General of the State of Oregon.

My attorneys of record have been Randall Vogt, Harrison Latto, George Kelly, Lisa Langford, Tomina Carter, Gregory Gudger, Jeff Price, Timothy Barnack and Ron Fishback, all of whom have been derelict and ineffective at their duties representing me. May shame forever reign on the City of Portland, Multnomah County, Delta Airlines and the State of Oregon. I am writing this letter so that I can have closure and so that you are aware of the events that happened to me in the justice system. Warmly and sincerely, Tyrone Waters. PS: Like my father once said to me on his deathbed, Ty, it's all on them."

And now here's been what's happening during the month of October, November and December 2010. I have been working at the Rose Garden Arena in Portland, Oregon. And on 10-12-2010, I ate lunch at a concession stand and became ill. I was transported via ambulance to Kaiser Sunnyside Medical Center from my place of employment due to an abdominal disorder that arose after eating a corndog at a concession stand at my place of employment at the Rose Garden Arena. I was evaluated in the emergency room at Kaiser Sunnyside and released. My time loss from work was from 10-12-2010 through 10-17-2010. And I was released for regular work duties on 10-18-2010. This is the second time that I have been food poisoned within the past year while working at the Rose Garden Arena. The Rose Garden Arena is also where the Portland Trailblazers play and also where other performing artists have performances. The management staff have refused to pay my Workman's Compensation claim and have been uncooperative in getting it paid. And they are also refusing to give me money for pain and suffering as a result of having been food poisoned.

On November 3, 2010, there was an incident at Kaiser Permanente Dental Office at N.E. Grand Dental Office in Portland, Oregon. A dental receptionist and dental assistant by the name of Kim, approached me and made the following comment, "We want you dead. We want you gone." I immediately got a hold of Grant Colby, the Dental Services Manager at that office and filed a complaint. And I also turned in a grievance. And Cindy Hollinger with Kaiser Permanente, Member

Relations and Grievance Administrator, reviewed my grievance and did nothing about it. Also Grant Colby, the Manager, the Dental Services Manager at that office, did nothing about the incident.

In the matter of Credit Concepts versus Tyrone Waters, the following letter was written November 2, 2010 to the Judge of small claims court, Lane County Oregon Court Building 125 East 8th Avenue, Eugene, Oregon 97401. "Regarding small claims court case number 70-10-21373, Honorable Judge, my name is Tyrone Waters. I am a disabled citizen on fixed income. I recently had my medical prescription drug coverage cut and it forces me to have prescription drug payments of over $500.00 a month. Because of that expense, I am unable to satisfy my obligations to Credit Concepts for a vehicle I had financed through them. The vehicle was repossessed and sold. There was a remaining balance and I was unable to negotiate with them a payment plan, due to the fact that I am on fixed income. I do not have the funds to pay the debt. I reside in Multnomah County Oregon. Because of the distance and the cost, I am unable to appear in person. I hope you will take this into consideration when rendering a judgment. Thank you for your time and consideration in this matter. Very respectfully, Tyrone Waters, 1725 S. E. Morrison, #2, Portland, Oregon 97214. Phone number 503-309-1679."

During the week of November 15th, 2010, my Kaiser Permanente health premium information and my Globe life insurance policy information have been stolen from my apartment.

When will they ever stop their destructive practices? I'm talking about the City, the County, the State and also members of the community and people in government. The harassment continues. It has not stopped. It is ongoing to this very day.

As of October 2010, I have resigned from the Rose Garden Arena and I am no longer employed there. I am still trying to get my Workman's Compensation claim resolved and have been unsuccessful.

Post script: I had to get a restraining order against my neighbor, Christine Dolly, who lives at 1310 S.E. Pine Street, Portland, Oregon

97214 for harassment, threats and intimidation. Also, during 2012 I became homeless, not by choice, and had to live in a homeless men's shelter in downtown Portland at Transition Projects Incorporated.

Also during 2012, I moved to the Patton Home in North Portland, which is run by Ecumenical Ministries. While living at the Patton Home, I experienced harassment, threats and intimidation. Some of the residents made comments saying they want me dead. I find this very unsettling to have to be experiencing such harassment in a religious community for housing.

In 2013, I finally found a place to live. And I am happy where I'm at currently. And I am enjoying life with my family and friends. Thank you for listening. Many blessings to you, wherever you may be. And I hope that you have been enlightened and educated about my experience.

[End of Volume 2]

[Volume 3]

Welcome to Volume 3. On December 9, 2013, I went to the Oregon Bureau of Labor and Industries Civil Rights Division to inquire about my file. I spoke with Donna Brown, Civil Rights Division, on 12-10- 2013 and indicated to her that I wanted a copy of my file. She said that she would send a request form. She sent me a request form dated 12-10-2013 with my name misspelled on the envelope, on the mailing envelope. She has Williams. And my last name is Waters. I tried to get a hold of Mary Claire, one of the investigators at the Civil Rights Division. I also tried to contact Christine Hammond, BOLi investigator, Bureau and Labor Industries supervisor. And then I spoke with Bureau of Labor and Industries Commissioner Jessie Bontecou. The following senior investigators were on the case investigating the wrongdoings. Their names are Chris Lynch, Senior Investigator, Civil Rights Division; Carrie Johnson, Senior Investigator, Civil Rights Division, all out of the Portland Office.

On August 21, 2012, I got a temporary stalking protective order against Christine Dolly, Case Number 1208-10303. She was also served with a stalking order by Multnomah County Sheriff's Officer Kristofferson, Eric; Badge #23232, is what it reads on this form. I signed my Bureau of Labor and Industries Civil Rights complaint on July 19, 2012. Prior to ... Or after that, I was homeless and staying at Transition Project downtown ... in downtown Portland. I became homeless on August 31st, 2012. The following staff harassed me while I was staying at Transition Projects: Tim, Damian and Andrew on the day shift, Jarrod and James on the swing shift, and Dale and Scott on the graveyard shift. I reported the harassment to Doreen, the Director of Transition Projects and she never got back to me. And I wound up leaving the homeless shelter because she did nothing about the harassment.

Some time later in 2013, I moved into the Patton Home, which is run by Ecumenical Ministries. While I was at the Patton Home, I was harassed and wound up leaving the Patton Home as well. The following letter was sent to Brian Cass, Manager of the Patton Home: "Dear Brian, This letter is confirm that I have vacated the property of the Patton Home, 4619 N. Michigan Avenue, #237 Portland, Oregon 97217-3168 effective August 9, 2013 due to you, your staff and other residents at the Patton Home's tireless efforts and all others involved in hostile lies, hatred and racism and conspiracy to commit attempted murder directed towards me. That's what lies, hatred and racism do. I am placing the key bob in the mailbox. Warmly, coldly, Tyrone Waters. Carbon copy Ecumenical Ministries to the Executive Director of Ecumenical Ministries."

People that were enemies and hated me at the Patton Home are as follows: All of the Patton Home staff, Joe Klosinger room #235, Bob room #225, Heather Allen room #216, Heather Davidson room #107. And I found out at a later date that she moved into my room, 237, after I left the Patton Home. Brian Lane room #115, Eric Berglund room #214 and Anna Hartwick room #213, all at the Patton Home, managed and owned and operated by Ecumenical Ministries and 1PM Management.

On June 27, 2012, I received a letter from Legal Aid Services of Oregon. It reads as follows: "Dear Mr. Waters, You contacted Legal

Aid recently because of a housing discrimination compliant. You allege that you have been harassed by your next door neighbors and other tenants in your complex because of your race and sexual orientation. You have reported several incidents to REACH Property Management, but you don't believe they have responded properly to your complaints. In addition, you have also made several police reports and reported incidents to your case manager at Home Forward. Some of your complaints are, your White neighbors have called you racist and homophobic names because you can hear them talking through the walls. They have intentionally allowed a pit bull to remain outside their door to intimidate you. And there have been several burglaries and attempted burglaries in your unit.

You have received two notices with cause as a tenant in your current housing on May 5, 2011 and October 7, 2011. You deny the allegations on both notices and responded to them in writing. You contacted Legal Aid after receiving the May 5th notice and received advice from this office on how to cure the notice and were given advice on what agency you should contact to file a housing discrimination and complaint to investigate your allegations. You also told me about incidents that occurred in your prior residence on S.E. Morrison Street address in 2010, which eventually led REACH to approve your request to relocate.

A meeting was held with Carrie Lewis, REACH property manager, her supervisor, Rachael, Tyrone White, case manager with Home Forward and Joe Nunn with Operation Clean Sweep. After discussing your behavior in response to threats and intimidation by your neighbor, eventually REACH agreed your request to transfer because you were suffering with paranoia due to your allegations of threats from your neighbor. Disability Rights of Oregon assisted you in a request for reasonable accommodations to transfer.

We have now completed our investigation. And after much consideration, it is our legal opinion that we do not have sufficient evidence to proceed to Court on your case. In the context of neighbor to neighbor harassment, the Fair Housing Act prohibits interference with any person in their enjoyment of the dwelling because of race or sexual orientation. Hostile comments and harassment because of race or sexual orientation case are covered by the Fair Housing Act.

And therefore, a landlord may be liable if he/she does make efforts to stop the behavior once he/she became aware of it. The law requires the landlord to take prompt, remedial action.

When you complained to Carrie Lewis about the neighbor in your prior apartment, a meeting was held to investigate your complaints. You were eventually transferred to your current apartment where, unfortunately, you have complained about continued harassment by different neighbors. I asked if you had supporting witnesses or statements. I talked to your uncle, who could not give supporting evidence other than what you told him. You told me your mother called the police to do a welfare check on you, but that is not the same as being a witness. I also spoke with Beth Englander from Disability Rights of Oregon. Although she believes that your neighbor at the Morrison Street Complex may have called you names and intimidated you, she explained there was nothing to prove a level of proof. Without supported evidence, makes it difficult to prove your accusations in Court.

Finally, I reviewed your file at Home Forward. It is clear that you did inform both Tyrone White and your current case manager, Rita Picarick about your housing discrimination complaint. Rita informed me that she did an investigation of your allegations about your current next door neighbor. Unfortunately, she told me that the preponderance of the evidence supported your neighbor's innocence of the accusations. No other details were provided about the neighbor. The incidents you have told me about which have occurred in your current unit, such as the burglaries, what you overheard your neighbor say through the walls but not clearly hearing your name mentioned, would be difficult to prove in Court. Also, the medication and items of food that was missing or stolen from you unit and spillage of garbage on your floor is not evidence of race or sexual orientation discrimination without independent evidence.

You should not have to live in fear of your neighbors or have to tolerate racial epithets in the place you live. It is our theory that the landlord has a duty to stop that behavior. However, the harder part of your case, involving statements you have overheard through the walls is not substantial enough for a property manager to inquire with your neighbors about. Other statements you overheard such as, oh, he doesn't want to talk to you, is not a racists statement on the surface, unless there were other racial-related circumstances which led up to this statement. But other statements you overheard such as, you're dead, is intimidating. But you have no supporting witnesses that those statements were directed to you.

Even in all the police reports ordered to persuade a Judge, we would most likely need supporting witnesses, evidence. And you told us there were no witnesses to the statements you have heard since being in your current housing. The statements you overheard your neighbors say, such as protect me from him, and we have a Black guy moving in, while extremely upsetting is still difficult to prove those are racial statements. If life-threatening statements are made to you, don't hesitate to call the police.

In 2010, while living in your former apartment, the neighbors racial harassment was supported by a letter written by your witness, Rita. Landlords have an obligation to stop the harassment once they are aware of it. REACH allowed you to transfer to the unit you are in now. And you are unaware if REACH took action against the neighbors who were harassing you and did not pursue their housing claims against REACH at that time.

Again, our decision not to pursue a Court case on your behalf is based only on a legal assessment of the claims and whether we think there is sufficient evidence to succeed at trial. I encourage you to obtain another legal opinion on your case. You should be aware that there are timelines in taking any legal action. An administrative housing discrimination compliant under the Fair Housing Act and State fair housing laws must be filed within one year of the date of the violation. You can contact the Bureau of Labor and Industries, BOLi, at 971-673-0764 to find out more about filing a housing discrimination complaint. If you are unable to write a summary of your allegations, if you contact BOLi be sure to make the intake person aware of your limitations.

A lawsuit under the Fair Housing Act and State Fair Housing laws must be filed within two years of the date of the discriminatory action. You do not need to file an administrative housing discrimination complaint before you file a lawsuit. You may have other claims that have shorter or longer timelines. You may want to call the Oregon State Bar's Lawyer Referral Program at 503-684-3763.

This letter will conclude our services for you in this matter. And your file will now be closed. If you are not satisfied with the manner of quality of service provided by Legal Aid Services of Oregon, you can request a copy of the grievance procedure. Please be aware that we will purge your file in five years. You are always welcome to call Legal Aid back for services in the future. Sincerely, Joyce Lowry, Paralegal, Christina Dirks, Attorney at Law."

The following Portland police officers have been involved in this matter: Officer [Pho Phing Gongsa?]; Badge #32938, Officer West Helfridge, Badge #29194; Officer Jason Mills, Badge #47777; Officer Mathew Jamison, Badge #31898; Officer Klinger, Badge #21705; Officer Kay Steward-Fox, Badge #47852; Officer Andrew Cofode, Badge #40928; Officer Steven Endicott, Badge #26710; Officer Chad Stensengard, Badge #43480; Officer Ladd, Badge #31811; Officer Brett Burton, Badge #43860.

I am the son of former Oregon State Senator Avel Gordly. All of the individuals mentioned, with the exception of former Oregon State Senator Avel Gordly, they all have a problem with former Oregon State Senator Avel Gordly's son. The harassment and hatred and bullying have been endless, and continues. As of the date of this recording, I have been residing at the Dawson Park Apartments in Portland, Oregon in North Portland.

On December 9th, 2013, I left a voice telephonic message for Disability Rights of Oregon, Executive Director Bob Joondeph. I authorized him verbally to turn over any and all documents they have in their possession pertaining to me, Tyrone Waters, and to give them to Lisa Loving, a reporter in the Portland area.

So my question is to you, if none of this supposedly happened and there's a spin doctor wanting to keep a spin and a twist on things, then why is it that the emergency room doctor at Kaiser Permanente on 8-20-2012 write a letter to the Judge saying, uTo Whom it May Concern, Mr. Tyrone Waters has medical conditions that are exacerbated by the anxiety he feels from his housing situation. He would greatly benefit from any assistance in protecting him from further harassment from his neighbors. Thank you. Signed Jess [Breet Congura ?], Medical Doctor, August 20, 2012, Kaiser Permanente Northwest Region."

And, why would my Aunt, Deidre Waters, write a letter to Multnomah County Circuit Court and say the following: "My name is Deidre Waters. On a recent visit to Portland I witnessed a Caucasian male leaving the apartment of my nephew, Tyrone Waters. He came out of Mr. Water's apartment to go right across into the apartment across the porch directly in front of Mr. Water's apartment. I asked Mr. Waters if he had company and he said, no. Sincerely, Deidre Waters."

And furthermore, why would Matt Reed of Transition Projects write a letter to the Judge dated September 27, 2012 that reads as follows.""Dear Honorable Judge of the Circuit Court, I met with Mr. Tyrone Waters and have gotten to know him as a resident of our program over the past month. Mr. Waters came to us because of an eviction from REACH housing due to harassment from his neighbors. As a resident in our program, we ask that he work towards permanent housing and that this eviction severely limits Mr. Water's options. I believe it is not his fault that his eviction occurred. And Mr. Waters would greatly benefit from having this eviction taken off of his record. Please consider this if it is within your power, or provide Mr. Waters an avenue to further pursue his case. Please consider Mr. Waters' request as well to make his harassment and stalking order against his former neighbors permanent, as he feels it to be dangerous to his mental, physical and spiritual wellbeing. If you have any further questions of me, contact me. Matt Reed, Transition Projects."

On October 1, 2012, paramedics were called to Transition Projects, run #4241986. In the paramedics report, "Your medical complaint today is burning eyes, blurry vision or conditions may be worse than it seems. Emergency medical service providers do not have all of the diagnostic tools needed to identify a serious medical problem. Specific risk you could potentially face by refusing today are not limited to unknown substance to your eyes.."Could have blindness, as a result of one of the homeless individuals at Transition Projects spraying shaving cream in my eyes.

As I continue to reside at the Dawson Park Apartments in Portland, Oregon, I am continually harassed by the upstairs neighbor in apartment 311. So I say to you, now that you know what has happened, what has been going on and what is continuing to go on, shame on the State of Oregon, shame on the Governor, shame on Multnomah County and it's Commissioners, shame on the City of Portland, the Mayor and City Commissioners. And for all of those State employees out there, that have gone down to the Capitol to protest their PERS retirement benefits being cut, shame on you as well because you did not do your job or carry out your duties faithfully to find discrimination, harassment, bullying in my case, as well as sexual harassment due to sexual orientation.

This is the type of activity that public officials and their family members are subjected to on a daily basis, as well as famous people in the entertainment industry. And it's time that it stop. We want to live normally, peacefully and not have you in our business wanting to know every single thing that we do in our lives. You should be concerned with what you do in your lives. Because all of what has happened is embarrassing to all of the individuals that carried out this horrific activity.

I am not going to settle with these people. I'm not interested in that. You can't put a price on what they have done to me. But what I am doing is putting everybody's name out there, exposing them for who they are, so that everybody knows who they are, what they drd and it's out there. And, let's hope that I don't have to do a volume four. Or if I do, maybe I'll have something good to say.

And now here are some audio excerpts from an interview that my mom, former Oregon State Senator Avel Gordly and I participated in. [Very poor audio quality]

Tyrone: Everybody in the family embraced me. I feel very blessed having [unintelligible].

Former Senator Gordly: [Inaudible]. And he shared with me, one day, that he [inaudible]. I remember putting my arms around him and saying, you're mine ... [chuckles] ... you know? We'll just go forward.

Tyrone: I felt released.

Former Senator Gordly: [Inaudible] afraid [inaudible]. This could be a hostile walk in the Portland community. Just be glad that [unintelligible] Black and we don't envy. And too, the fear that I've felt sometimes towards your safety. And at the same time, I know that he is part of the community that is [inaudible]. Our church family, of course, [inaudible].

Tyrone: Having a pastor who is loving, caring, nonjudgmental is very important to me. It makes me feel more welcomed, accepted.

Former Senator Gordly: There is a stereotype still operating about the African American church being an unwelcome place for [inaudible]. And I want to call it what it is. I think it's a stereotype. I mean, every

church that we've went in, they're in the choir. They're playing the music. They may even be preaching. So it is a stereotype, meaning we call it for what it is. We keep breaking it down.

We come from a family of community [members?]. And what I want for our family is that they be able to [inaudible]that we are a part of building what Martin Luther King, Jr. called [inaudible],a community that embraces all races [inaudible]potentially. What I love about Ty to be [courage and intelligence?], intelligence and courage of God.

Tyrone: I'm just thankful for all the support ... [chuckles] ... that she has given me, being a mom and a friend. And someone who cares and tries to understand me. [End of taped interview]

I don't want to up-end. But let's not pretend. So let's keep it real.

Tyrone: [Recorded segment] Here's a meditation exercise that you can practice daily. First, find your place, get in the meditation position.

Relax, shut your eyes and take a few deep breathes. Now repeat to yourself, my body is whole and healthy. I am calm and loving. I am prosperous and successful. Repeat these ideas over and over until they take the place of the negative conviction that may be in your mind right now. [Unintelligible] power. You are now becoming that perfect image you want to be. And always know, no matter what you endure, always be forgiving. That you have a pleasant morning, afternoon or evening, wherever you may be. And many blessings to you. [End of recorded segment]

And sometimes you just have to accept life on life's terms and go the distance.

[End Volume 3]

[Volume 4]

Welcome to the 2014 edition of Volume Four, You Would Be Paranoid If Too If This Happened To You. in 2014 and beyond, I'm asking everyone, regardless of race, color, including military veterans and family members to boycott Delta Airlines and to divest, not invest, in City of Portland, Oregon, Multnomah County, Oregon and State of Oregon bonds. And to boycott Kaiser Permanente of Oregon healthcare plans because the mean-spiritedness against me continues, including my phone being wire tapped and electronic warfare, mind control, psychic warfare being used against me. It is very real. And the technology exists. And you're not crazy if that's what you believe is happening to you. Some people have killed themselves over it being done to them.

Some State of Oregon employees that work at the Oregon State Hospital have called my CDs unorthodox. And also know there are City of Portland and Multnomah County and State of Oregon, as well as Kaiser Permanente employees that live in my building. My story is what it is. And know that's what they do when they consider you an enemy.

Hopefully, by you listening to this series of CDs, you will be inspired to have the courage to make life changes, no matter how difficult they may seem to be able to achieve, when it comes to mental health and civil rights. And also that you will be enabled to release any anger and be forgiving in your heart and mind, and be more open and receptive to a greater love for one another as we are all One, simply put. And always know there's strength in numbers when you get ready to unite and take a stand. May you have healing, blessings and good health. And thank you for listening.

[End of "You Would Be Paranoid Too If This Happened To You."]

TER
NATIONAL
PEACE
MESSAGE
WRITTEN BY
INTERNATIONAL
AUTHOR TY AGUAS
IN TIJAUNA, B.C.
2015

Tyrone Waters

CIRCULATION OVER 675,000
MEMBER OF THE AUDIT BUREAU OF CIRCULATIONS
PRINTED IN THE UNITED STATES

HOLA~HALO~CIAO ~
BONJOUR ~ PRIVET~
ASIAN KOREAN~
JAPANESE~ PRIVIT
HEALING TO THE ABOVE

PSALMOS:18
SELAH IN THE
GRAZI
JESUS CHRISTO
SELAH en el
GRAZI
JESUS CHRISTO

HIGHEST

MARRIOTT
TIJUANA
MARRIOTT.COM

ESCAPE FAMILY PACKAGE

- Habitación Standard de Lujo
- Desayuno Buffet para dos adultos y dos menores de doce años
- Estacionamiento para un automóvil
- 10% de descuento en tabaquería

$2,519.23 M.N. precio por noche

ESCAPE ROMANCE PACKAGE

- Habitación Standard de Lujo
  Desayuno Buffet para dos adultos
- Botella de Chambroulet
- Fresas smoking 10 piezas
- Estacionamiento para un automóvil

$3,192.00 M.N. precio por noche

MAGNO PAQUETE

- Habitación Standard de Lujo
- Desayuno Buffet para dos adultos
- Estacionamiento para un automóvil

$1,927.80 M.N. precio por noche

· 209 HABITACIONES CON CORREO DE VOZ, CAJA DE SEGURIDAD, CAFETERA Y MINIBAR · ROOM SERVICE, 24 HORAS · PISOS EJECUTIVOS · TABAQUERÍA · DELI CAFÉ · BUSINESS CENTE · SALONES PARA CONVENCIONES Y EVENTOS SOCIALES · RESTAURANTE CONDIMENTO · GREAT ROOM · INTERNET INALÁMBRICO.

~~FOR INTERNATIONAL MESSAGE OF PEACE AND UNDERSTANDING~~

SOME PEOPLE HAVE THE ABILITY TO ALTER PUBLIC SPACE IN UGLY WAYS THIS PRINCIPLE IS THE KEY TO UNDERSTANDING ALL HIERARCHIAL SYSTEMS AND THERFORE A BETTER UNDERSTANDING OF THE WHOLE STRUCTURE OF AMERICA THE STATE OF OREGON PEOPLE SHOULD BE APPALLED AT THE STATE OF OREGONS PUBLIC WEALTH THAT CAUSES ENVIORNMENTAL MISSUNDERSTANDING DO WE AS A PEOPLE POSSESS THE COURAGE AND THE CHARACTER TO ADDRESS A PROBLEM WHERE PEOPLE ARE HOMELESS POORER AND HAVE FOUND IT NATURAL TO UNCORRECT YOU ARE ONLY HUMAN FLESH AND THE CANDLE CAN BURN AT BOTH ENDS BY THOSE INDIVIDUALS THAT CHOOSE TO PARTAKE FOR THOSE WHO HAVE THE STOMACHE FOR IT LET US PART THE FORMALDAHYDE CURTAIN AND EXPOSE THE TRUTH FOR WHAT IT IS THERES A LIST OF FAMILIES INDIVIDUALS HOUSEHOLDS AND THE LOTTERY REMAINS OPEN TO WHO BECOMES HOMELESS SO LONG AS WE UNDERSTAND THE PROCESS AND THE IMPLICATIONS AS WELL AS THE EXEMPLIFICATIONS TO WHO REMAINS EXEMPT AND ALLOWED TO CONTINUE SUCH PRACTICES NO MATTER HOW CLANDESTINE SUBTLE HATEFUL OR BULLYING A COLLABORATIVE OF AN ACTIVITY FOR SOME ITS OPEN FOR DISCUSSION FOR CHANGE TO PROCESS IT WORLD WIDE MULTI LINGUAL BECAUSE PEOPLE THAT ARE HOMELESS AS WELL AS HOMELESS VETERANS AND THE MENTALLY ILL CAN ENRICH OUR LIVES I HAVE TRIED TO HELP PEOPLE BUT THAT IS NOT GOOD ENOUGH WE ARE ALL HUMAN BEINGS AT DAYS END IN THE LIGHT INTO DARKNESS

FOR EACH DISAPPROVAL FOR EACH DISSAPOINTMENT ABOVE GROUND ABOVE A RIVER A RIVER WITHIN STILL ALIVE NOT DEAD BUT STILL ABLE UNTIL GONE TO WHAT IS NOT AND WILL NOT BE ACCEPTABLE OR TOLLERABLE

SOME SUBTLE HOWEVER CRASS EXAMPLES OF SO CALLED BLIND INSTINCT WHILE IN THE NOW IT MAY SUIT THE POWERS THAT BE AND THEIR IMAGE AND FURTHER REQUIRES THE CONCERTED EFFORTS OF A TEAM OF HIGHER DISCIPLINED INDIVIDUALS BOTH PROFESSIONAL AND UN PROFESSIONAL I AM HOPEFUL THAT YOU LEARN THAT BECAUSE SEX LIES CONVERSATION AND WHAT IS PRACTICED BY SOME PEOPLE WHO WANT TO SPREAD PROPOGANDA AS A SUBTLE FORM OF BULLYING WHEN THEY SHOULD BE AFRAID OF NOTHING THESE INDIVIDUALS ARE THE ONES WHO CLIMB A WALL WHETHER ITS REAL INVISIBLE AND TAKE A BOW AT THE TOP THIS IS NOT ONLY STAGGERING BUT QUESTIONS THE REASONING OF I DON'T WANT TO KNOW YOU DIDN'T KNOW NOW YOU KNOW THERE ARE PEOPLE WHOM WILL ALWAYS FIND A JUSTIFIABLE IN THEIR OWN EYES WAY TO DO WRONG AND IF MISMANAGED THEY WOULD BE LEFT WITH NOTHING I APOLOGIZE FOR NOTHING TASK DO NOT COME EASILY BUT TO BOYCOTT AN EVIL PROCESS DOESIS$$$........

TY WATERS

December 16, 2015

MULTNOMAH
MDI
DEFENDERS
INCORPORATED

YEON BUILDING
522 S.W. 5TH AVENUE
SUITE 1000
PORTLAND, OREGON 97204
multnomahdefenders.org
(503) 226-3083
FAX (503) 226-0107

Tyrone Waters
6805 NE Broadway
Portland, Oregon 97213

RE: State v. Waters
      15CC05146;   Civil Commitment Appeal

Dear Mr. Waters:

I received this address is location to send your correspondence. Attached is a copy of the legal brief in your appeal. Please contact me if you have any questions at 503-226-3083, ext. 115.

Sincerely,

Eric Deitrick,
Attorney at Law
MULTNOMAH DEFENDERS, INC.

IN THE COURT OF APPEALS OF THE STATE OF OREGON

In the Matter of T.W., Alleged to be a Person with Mental Illness.	)))	Multnomah County Circuit Court No. 15CC05146
STATE OF OREGON,	))	A160465
Respondent,	))	
v.	))	APPELLANT'S CONFIDENTIAL OPENING BRIEF
T.W.,	))	CONFIDENTIAL UNDER ORS 426.160
Appellant.	)	

Appeal from Judgment and Order of the Circuit Court for Multnomah County
Honorable E. Fithian-Barrett, Judge Pro Tempore

ERIC J. DEITRICK #052322
Multnomah Defenders, Inc.
522 SW Fifth Avenue #1000
Portland, Oregon 97204
(503) 226-3083
edeitrick@multnomahdefenders.org
Attorney for Appellant

ELLEN F. ROSENBLUM #753239
Attorney General
PAUL SMITH #001870
Solicitor General
1162 Court Street NE
Salem, Oregon 97301
(503) 378-4402
Attorneys for Respondent

10/2015

TABLE OF CONTENTS

The court erred by ruling that appellant was a mentally ill person when it concluded that appellant was a danger to himself and others.

APPELLANT'S CONFIDENTIAL OPENING BRIEF

STATEMENT OF THE CASE

Nature of the Proceedings

This is an appeal from a circuit court order committing appellant to the custody of the Oregon Health Authority for a period not to exceed 180 days. Appellant seeks to have this court reverse the order because the record lacks clear and convincing evidence that he was a person with a mental illness at the time of the hearing.

Nature of the Order

The orders were based upon a finding that appellant was mentally ill, and was not willing and able to participate in treatment on a voluntary basis. (ER-1).

Jurisdiction

The statutory basis of appellate jurisdiction is ORS 19.205.

Notice of Appeal

The notice of appeal was filed on October 2, 2015 from orders entered on September 14, 2015.

Question Presented

Does the record contain clear and convincing evidence that appellant was a danger to himself or others?

Summary of Argument

Appellant does not dispute that he has a mental disorder. However, the record lacks clear and convincing evidence that he was a danger to himself or others at the time of the hearing.

Appellant's singular threat to the Governor's office cannot justify commitment as it lacks an overt act and was made three months prior to the commitment hearing when appellant was in another state.

And while appellant dressed and described himself as a bounty hunter, concluding that appellant would harm himself or others is speculation as the record lacks a foundation from which to predict an actual serious physical injury in the near future. To the contrary, appellant merely gathers information on people whom he perceives are breaking the law, and then turns that information over to law enforcement. Appellant has never attempted to arrest or detain anyone, and the record contains no evidence that this had ever led to a physical confrontation.

Statement of Facts

Appellant is a 49 year old man whose diagnoses include schizophrenia, paranoid type, and schizoaffective disorder, manic type. Tr 6, 53, 83. When ill and untreated, appellant experiences delusions, disorganized speech, irritability, pressured speech, and grandiosity. Tr 7. He also experiences paranoid delusions that people are trying to harm and kill him. Tr 8, 65.

Appellant's mother is former State Senator Avel Gordly, and she recalls him first receiving a mental health diagnosis in the 1990s following his service in the Navy. Tr 53. In 2001, appellant was shot with bean bag rounds outside of his home by Portland Police Officers. Tr 54. At the time of the shooting, appellant believed people wanted to harm and kill him. Tr 64. Following that event, appellant spent time at the Oregon State Hospital. Tr 54.

Appellant had periods of success thereafter where he was stable and receiving medication. Tr 55. He worked as a counselor at Cascadia Behavioral Healthcare for four years. Tr 55. He served on the Board for Disability Rights Oregon. Tr 85. He treated with the Veteran's Administration. Tr 56. In the fall of 2014, appellant was assigned a new counselor at the Veteran's Administration, who in turn changed the medication plan. Tr 56. At that time, appellant's stability eroded. Tr 56.

In September or October of 2014, appellant left Portland and traveled by train to Canada with the hope of obtaining political asylum. Tr 56, 98. Appellant feared living in the United States as a black gay man with mental illness. Tr 58. In April of 2015, appellant was in a Canadian immigration detention center pending an asylum hearing. Tr 58, 81. His request was denied, and he was transferred back to the state of Washington. Tr 81.

Following removal from Canada, appellant traveled south to Mexico by train with the hope of obtaining asylum there. Tr 76-77. He also spent some time in San Diego, California, where several things happened. On June 15, 2015, appellant phoned the constituent line of Governor Kate Brown, identified himself, and left a voicemail in which he used profanity and threatened to kill her. Tr 18, 20. It is undisputed that appellant was in California when this call was placed to Oregon. Tr 25. Oregon State Police Trooper Chris Schinnerer stated that the Governor's office receives 8 to 12 such calls a month.

In addition, appellant stated he was assaulted five times in San Diego. Tr 92. The record contains no information about whether appellant suffered an injury, let alone a serious physical injury in San Diego. Later that summer, in July, appellant was placed on a hold in San Diego, although it appears to have been lifted quickly. Tr 113.

On September 4, appellant traveled by train to Portland. Tr 32. After traveling to Canada and Mexico, appellant wanted to obtain an enhanced identification card. Tr 34. The enhanced identification card offered appellant the benefits of a passport, but was less expensive. Tr 117. Appellant needed his birth certificate to obtain the enhanced identification card. Tr 49. With the enhanced identification card, appellant believed he could legally enter and remain in Canada or Mexico. Tr 34, 117-18.

Upon nearing Portland, Portland Police received a call from the Amtrak conductor that there was a person of concern on the train. Tr 32. Sgt. Burley of Portland Police Bureau responded to the Amtrak station, as did several other people, including appellant's mother. Tr 33, 64. Appellant exited the train wearing a white uniform with a badge, and a duty belt that included pepper spray, a flashlight, and handcuffs. Tr 33. All of these objects are things that can be purchased by the public. Tr 47.

Appellant was waiting for a cab when Sgt. Burley approached him. Tr 33. The two spoke for one to two hours. Tr 36. Appellant said he was a bounty hunter and volunteer security for Amtrak. Tr 36, 38. Based on appellant's dress and statement about being a bounty hunter, a mental health hold was placed on appellant and he was taken to the hospital. Tr 45.

During the hospitalization, appellant was cooperative. Tr 7. He was not placed in seclusion and no restraints were ever used. Tr 14. Dr. Wilson, a psychiatric resident who treated appellant, opined that appellant was a danger to himself and others because his belief that he was a bounty hunter would put him in harm's way. Tr 10.

At the time of the hearing, appellant wanted to be discharged so that he could obtain his enhanced identification and travel to Mexico or Canada. Tr 118, 130. While holding himself out as a bounty hunter, there was no evidence that appellant had ever been arrested or detained. Tr 73. Nor was there evidence that appellant had ever arrested or detained anyone. Tr 73. To the contrary, appellant has consistently avoided physical confrontations and has chosen to contact legitimate law enforcement when he perceived a threatening or criminal event. Tr 111.

In San Diego, when appellant felt as though he had been assaulted, he contacted the San Diego Police Department. Tr 93, 110. Before traveling by train to Portland, he contacted Amtrak security. Tr 94. When appellant perceived hostility on the train, he contacted the FBI. Tr 107. Sgt. Burley testified that appellant merely gathers information on people whom he perceives are breaking the law, and then turns that information over to law enforcement. Tr 38-39. Appellant was not suicidal and did not want to harm anyone. Tr 119.

ASSIGNMENT OF ERROR

The court erred by ruling that appellant was a person with mental illness when it concluded that appellant was a danger to himself and others.

Preservation of Error

Appellant argued that the evidence was insufficient for involuntary commitment:

> And Your Honor, Mr. Waters is asking to be discharged today, and be allowed to leave the hospital. There's no evidence in the record to support the Court making a finding under the basic needs prongs, so I'm not going to address that. With regards danger to others, this is kind of an interesting fact pattern based on the case law. Everybody seems to agree that there's – there's some heightened words, language, sometimes when Mr. Waters has been quite upset, quite frustrated, quite angry, and has left phone messages. However, he – it was – it was very clear that he wasn't in the state of Oregon when that was left upon their investigation . . . So not only was it only speech, which is protected, even for people that are mentally ill. But there was no additional engagement, attempts to engaged with the Governor . . . We don't have anything of that, we just have one voicemail that was made at a time when he was not in the State of Oregon.

* * *

And with regards to harm's way, it's kind of an interesting fact patter, because Mr. Waters really doesn't want to encounter other people. He wants to avoid confrontation. He describes his actions assisting law enforcement and as what he described as a voluntary bounty hunter, but the way he described them were really that the circumstances happened, and he has a citizen followed up and called the authorities.

* * *

So it would be my position that under this – under this record, the Court cannot make the – the State has not met its burden with regard to either the danger to others, or the dangerous to self under the harm's way theory, and it would be too speculative for the Court to make the finding for harm's way.

Tr 130-34.

The court concluded that appellant was a person with mental illness by concluding that he was a danger to himself and others but did not elaborate or provide explanations. Tr 134.

Standard of Review

Unless this court exercises its discretion to review *de novo*, it is bound by the trial court's findings of historical fact that are supported by evidence in the record and it reviews the trial court's dispositional conclusions that are predicated on those findings as a matter of law. *State v. B. B.*, 240 Or

App 75, 77, 245 P3d 697 (2010).

Argument

A court may order involuntary commitment of a person for up to 180 days if the court finds clear and convincing evidence that the person is mentally ill, meaning that (1) he has a mental disorder; (2) he is dangerous to herself or others, or is unable to provide for his basic personal needs and is not receiving necessary car for health and safety; and (3) the mental disorder is the cause of his dangerousness or of his inability to provide or receive care to meet basic personal needs. *State v. Puha*, 208 Or App 453, 460, 144 P3d 1044 (2006); ORS 426.005(1)(e); ORS 426.130(1)(b). The determination must focus on his condition *at the time of the hearing*. *State v. Lucas*, 31 Or App 947, 950, 571 P2d 1275 (1977) (emphasis added).

1. <u>Danger to Others (Threat to Governor's Office)</u>

A conclusion that a mental disorder causes a person to be a danger to others requires clear and convincing evidence proving that it is highly probable at the time of the hearing that a person has a mental disorder that will cause the person to engage in violence against others in the near future. *State v. M. R.*, 225 Or App 569, 575-76, 202 P3d 221 (2009). Isolated incidents do not support a finding of dangerousness. *State v. D.R.*, 239 Or

App 576, 583, 244 P3d 916 (2010). Evidence of verbal threats of violence is insufficient if the threats are not accompanied by any overt act to follow through with the threat or if they are not made under circumstances that make actual future violence highly likely. *State v. D.R.K.*, 216 Or App 120, 122, 171 P3d 998 (2007).

In *D.R.K.*, the appellant had been stabbing kitchen knives into the ground shortly before the involuntary hospitalization, and she had also threatened to cut off her mother's legs and kill her. *Id.* This court noted that the record lacked evidence about the circumstances under which the threat was made, and there was no evidence suggesting she would follow through with the acts. *Id.* at 123.

In *State v. K.L.*, 220 Or App 647, 188 P3d 395 (2008), this court reversed an involuntary commitment predicated upon the appellant's threats to her neighbor and neighbor's children. This court reversed, noting that, although the tenor and imagery of the threats was disturbing, the record lacked evidence that the threats would come to fruition. *Id.* at 656.

Here, appellant made one threat to the Governor's office via telephone voicemail message. While the tenor of the threat may have been disturbing, it was made on June 15; the commitment hearing occurred three months later on September 14. The threat was made while appellant was in California. In the three months following the voicemail, there is no evidence that appellant took any overt act or repeated the threat.

This court has acknowledged that it is tempting to err on the side of caution when facing a risk of violence because no judge can ever be sure that a person who has been committed will not engage in violence, but it has also noted that such reasoning unlawfully shifts the burden of proof away from the state. *State v. Hitt*, 179 Or App 563, 573, 41 P3d 434 (2002). The singular telephonic threat in this case lacks any overt act and circumstances from which one could predict violence was highly likely in the near future.

2. <u>Danger to Self (Bounty Hunter)</u>

This court has required a rigorous proof threshold to establish that a person is dangerous to self. *State v. R.E.*, 248 Or App 481, 490, 273 P3d 341 (2012). A decision that appellant is a danger to self requires extraordinarily persuasive evidence in the record that his mental condition at the time of the hearing made it highly probable that he would engage in conduct that would result in actual serious physical injury to him in the near future. *See B.B.*, 240 Or App at 82-83 (stating standard). Here, there was no evidence that appellant was suicidal. And while the circuit court did not explain how it reached its conclusion, the parties arguments to the court were based on whether appellant was a danger to himself by placing himself in "harm's way." Tr 128, 133.

A person can be deemed dangerous to self if not suicidal only if he has established a pattern in the past of taking certain actions that lead to self-destructive conduct and begins to follow the pattern again. *B.B.*, 240 Or App at 83. However, the danger cannot be speculative. *Id.* Such restraint comports with the fundamental principle that the power to civilly commit a person must not be used "as a 'paternalistic vehicle' to 'save people from themselves.'" *Id.*

This court has said that it is not the state's prerogative to use the civil commitment statutes to interfere with a person's choice of lifestyle even if that choice is not one that everyone would make. *State v. Gjerde*, 147 Or App 187, 192, 935 P2d 1224 (1997). "Delusional or eccentric behavior – even that may be inherently risky – is not necessarily sufficient to warrant commitment." *B.B.*, 240 Or App at 83.

This court has also consistently reversed orders of involuntary commitment when the "danger to self" was based on a risk of placing one's self in "harm's way." *See B.B.*, 240 Or App at 83 ("Our decisions addressing putative 'danger to self' commitments based on 'harm's way' concerns highlight the proper application of the foregoing legal principles.") The use of the term "harm's way" demonstrates the circuit court's inability to identify a highly probable and non-speculative danger as required by this court.

In *State v. D.R.*, 183 Or App 520, 52 P3d 1123 (2002), this court reversed an order of involuntary commitment for insufficient evidence that the alleged mentally ill person placed themselves in "harm's way." The person had a mental disorder, was not taking their medication, wandered the streets, and stepped off of the curb into the road. Although the individual wandered the streets frequently, this court noted that there was no evidence that the person's behavior had ever led to an injury. *Id* at 525.

In *State v. T.R.O.*, 208 Or App 686, 145 P3d 350 (2006), this court reversed an order of involuntary commitment for insufficient evidence that the alleged mentally ill person placed themselves in "harm's way." The person suffered from schizophrenia, hallucinations, and had poor judgment. Before his most recent hospitalization, he had a tendency to walk into other people's homes. This court noted that there was insufficient evidence about the number of times the person engaged in that behavior, and insufficient evidence that the person was likely to repeat that behavior. *Id.* at 693.

Here, the record contains evidence that appellant postured as a bounty hunter. However, there is no evidence that appellant has ever physically confronted anyone. While holding himself out as a bounty hunter, there was no evidence that appellant had ever arrested or detained anyone. Tr 73. Nor was there evidence that appellant had ever been arrested or detained. Tr 73.

To the contrary, appellant has consistently avoided physical confrontations and has chosen to contact legitimate law enforcement when he perceived a threatening or criminal event, including the San Diego Police Department, Amtrak security, and the FBI. Tr 93, 94, 107, 111. Appellant did testify that he was previously assaulted in San Diego. However, this court requires evidence of physical injury to be "serious" and "life-threatening." *B.B.*, 240 Or App at 85. Here, the record lacks any evidence about what type of injury appellant experienced, if any.

This court itself has acknowledged that predicting human behavior is an inherently speculative endeavor, *State v. Simon*, 180 Or App 255, 263, 42 P3d 374 (2002), and it has declared that a court may not commit a person based upon speculation about what a person "might" or "could" do. *State v.*

M. R., 225 Or App at 576. "When the legislature imposed a burden of persuasion of clear and convincing, or highly probable, evidence, it sought to ensure that involuntary commitment and the deprivation of liberty that accompanies it would not occur except when based on evidence of 'extraordinary persuasiveness.'" *Id.*

In this case, the record lacks clear and convincing evidence of a pattern of actions that previously led to actual serious physical injury. Appellant's eccentric behavior as a bounty hunter is insufficient to support a finding that appellant faced a highly probable threat of serious physical injury in the near future is speculation.

CONCLUSION

Appellant does not dispute that he has a mental disorder. However, appellant submits that he cannot be involuntarily committed simply for having a mental disorder. Appellant respectfully requests this court issue an order vacating the circuit court's order of commitment as the record does not contain clear and convincing evidence that he was a danger to himself or others at the time of the hearing.

Respectfully submitted,

Eric J. Deitrick #052322
Multnomah Defenders, Inc.
522 SW Fifth Avenue #1000
Portland, Oregon 97204
(503) 226-3083
edeitrick@multnomahdefenders.org
Attorney for Appellant

EXCERPT OF RECORD INDEX

IN THE CIRCUIT COURT OF THE STATE OF OREGON
FOR THE COUNTY OF MULTNOMAH
Family Law Department

In the Matter of) No. 15cc05146

Tyrone Waters)

Alleged to be a Mentally Ill Person,) GENERAL JUDGMENT

By virtue of a notification of mental illness, a citation was issued and served upon the above named. A hearing was thereupon held this date, in which the following named persons appeared:

A. The above named who is alleged to be mentally ill.

B. _MPD - E. Weefield_, appointed counsel for the above named.

C. DEPUTY DISTRICT ATTORNEY, representing the State's interest.

D. Sand Carlyle and ~~Dr Stephanie Korff~~, examiners.
    Linda O'Malia

THE COURT HEREBY ORDERS AS FOLLOWS:

☐ The notification of mental illness is dismissed and the above named person is discharged.

☒ The Court finds upon clear and convincing evidence the above named suffers from a mental disorder and
- _X_ is dangerous to others.
- _X_ is dangerous to self.
- ___ is unable to provide for basic personal needs and is not receiving such care as is necessary for health or safety.
- ___ has stipulated to a civil commitment.

☒ The Court further finds the above named is either unwilling, unable or unlikely to participate in treatment on a voluntary basis, and a conditional release is either unavailable or not in the above named person's best interest. It is therefore ordered the above named person be committed and promptly delivered to the Mental Health Division for a period not to exceed 180 days. If applicable, conditions of the outpatient commitment are attached.

☐ The above named person is conditionally released pursuant to ORS 426.125 to
____ whose address and telephone number are
_______________________________________ for a period not to exceed 180 days. The conditions of such release are attached hereto

IT IS FURTHER ORDERED the Multnomah County Department of Community and Family Services, Behavioral Health Division Commitment Services, release to the court appointed counsel for the committed person, upon request, the location, or last known location of the committed person.

For purposes of appeal, the Multnomah County Attorney may have access to this circuit court file.

DATED this 14 September 2015.

____
CIRCUIT COURT JUDGE (signature)

L Fitman-Barrett
____
CIRCUIT COURT JUDGE (printed)

General Judgment

Page 1 of 1

CERTIFICATE OF SERVICE AND COMPLIANCE WITH ORAP 5.05

I certify that this brief is printed in type not smaller than 14 point and that its 3,153 words comply with the word-count limitation in ORAP 5.05.

I further certify that Appellant's Opening Brief was filed with the Appellate Court Administrator by eFiling the document on December 14, 2015 and directing the motion to the Appellate Court Administrator, Appellate Courts Records Section, 1163 State Street, Salem, Oregon 97301.

I further certify that, upon receipt of the confirmation email stating that the document has been accepted by the eFiling system, this Appellant's Opening Brief will be eServed pursuant to ORAP 16.45 (regarding electronic service on registered eFilers) on Paul Smith #001870, Solicitor General, attorney for Respondent.

Eric J. Deitrick #052322
Multnomah Defenders, Inc.
522 SW Fifth Avenue #1000
Portland, Oregon 97204
(503) 226-3083
edeitrick@multnomahdefenders.org
Attorney for Appellant

This is What They Had To Say about Me

By Author

Rev. Dr. Tyrone Waters

Historical Events

Dr. Tyrone Waters, D.D., DRS.
rev.dr.tywaters@gmail.com
503-715-6998
In the United States
6544 N.E. Broadway St. #761
Portland, OR 97213
U. S. NAVY
VETERAN

```
LOCAL TITLE: Discharge Summary
  ADMIN DATE: SEP 05, 2015          DISCH. DATE: OCT 15, 2015
STANDARD TITLE: DISCHARGE SUMMARY
  DICT DATE: SEP 29, 2015@16:50      ENTRY DATE: SEP 29, 2015@16:51:02
DICTATED BY: DEMARCO,EMILY T         ATTENDING: CORNEJO,BRANDON J
   URGENCY: routine                     STATUS: COMPLETED
```

    *** Discharge Summary Has ADDENDA ***

ATTENDING PHYSICIAN: Brandon Cornejo

PRIMARY CARE PROVIDER AND FACILIITY: Not assigned

PRINCIPAL DIAGNOSIS:
Psychosis NOS

DSM5 DIAGNOSES:
Psychosis NOS

OTHER DIAGNOSES TREATED OR IMPACTING TREATMENT THIS ADMISSION:
None

PROCEDURES PERFORMED AT THIS HOSPITAL DURING CURRENT ADMISSION:
Recreational therapy
Psychotherapy
Medication titration

SUMMARY:
(ABBREVIATED HPI, PE, AND PERTINENT LABS)

From excellent admit note on 9/5/2015 by Dr. Eric Weathers:
"Tyrone Waters is a 49 year old man with history of
psychosis, depression, and anxiety who was brought to the OHSU ED by ambulance
(as the VA ED is apparently on ambulance divert) from an Amtrak train he took
from San Diego to Portland. Reportedly, he was wearing a security guard uniform
and in possession of handcuffs and pepper spray on this train, claiming that he
was a bounty hunter and security guard and threatening female passengers. In
addition, a vehicle was reportedly found at the San Diego airport with the
patient's ID and multiple firearms inside. He received ziprasidone 20 mg IM en
route to the emergency room.

In the OHSU ED, Mr. Waters was generally uncooperative with assessments, though
did endorse the possibly paranoid belief that there was a gang following him and
forcing him to "do things" as well as persecutory ideation that people on the
train were rude to him and called him "the n-word." He was described by
providers in the OHSU ED as irritable, agitated, and aggressive with rapid,
pressured speech. He received lorazepam 1 mg PO x2 in the ED.

On arrival to 5C, Mr. Waters initially agreed to provide his history and allow a
physical examination. However, he would only answer questions initially with an

<table>
<tr><td>PATIENT NAME AND ADDRESS (Mechanical Imprinting, if available)

WATERS,TYRONE X
6805 NE BROADWAY
PORTLAND, OREGON 97213</td><td>VISTA Electronic Medical Documentation
Printed at PORTLAND VA MEDICAL CENTER</td></tr>
</table>

exaggerated "no" and then look away again. After a few questions, primarily attempts to obtain his medical history, medications, allergies, and substance use, he began to respond only by directing us loudly to leave his room.

Given that patient was felt to be a danger to others and placed on a hospital hold, and was refusing to provide any information, his next of kin (mother, Joyce Gordly) was contacted, who was able to verify some of the patient's history as well as current circumstances. She reported that Mr. Waters was diagnosed with schizophrenia "many years ago" and that he has reported hearing voices. He was under psychiatric care here at the VA until January 2014 at which time he elected to receive health care services at Kaiser. Reportedly, Mr. Waters did not feel that he was receiving culturally sensitive care as a homosexual and a black man. In September 2014, perhaps in an attempt to get away from this type of persecution, the patient moved first to Washington State then to Canada. He was jailed from January to April and then deported back to the United States. He traveled to San Diego to be near the Mexican border, where he has been staying under unknown circumstances until traveling back this week to Portland in an attempt to obtain his birth certificate in order to get a passport and be able to travel across the border legally."

MSE and PE from admit note:
General appearance: middle-aged black man laying on his bed, dressed in hospital scrubs, in no apparent distress
Behavior and psychomotor activity: no tremor or other abnormal movements observed, no apparent psychomotor agitation; patient was uncooperative with interview
Language and speech: fluent and coherent with normal rate, volume, rhythm, and prosody
Thought process: difficult to assess given brevity of responses; patient answered questions linearly, though this answer was generally just "no"
Thought Content: difficult to assess given brevity of responses; however, did evidence some paranoid ideation as patient accused that we have an order to kill out on him.
Mood: not assessed
Affect: irritable
Judgment: poor
Insight: poor
Cognition: not formally assessed, patient does recognize that he is in a hospital

PHYSICAL EXAM:
Gen: middle-aged black man laying on his bed, dressed in hospital scrubs, in no apparent distress
HEENT: patient refused exam
Lungs: breathing effortlessly, no audible wheezes
CV: patient refused exam
Abd: patient refused exam
Ext: patient refused exam; no obvious skin rash or deformity of extremities observed
Neuro:

VISTA Electronic Medical Documentation
Printed at PORTLAND VA MEDICAL CENTER

-CN: no facial asymmetry or dysarthria observed
-Strength: patient was able to move all extremities freely
-Reflexes: patient refused exam
-Cerebellar/coordination: patient refused exam
-Sensation: patient refused exam
-Gait: patient refused exam

labs from OHSU were pertinent for:
UA inconsistent with infection (<1 WBC, no bacteria, LE negative) and no glucosuria or proteinuria; UDS pan-negative; negative; CMP: pertinent for sodium 146, potassium 3.9, chloride 112, glucose 107, calcium 7.9, albumin 2.7; *TSH 0.42

HOSPITAL COURSE:
Mr. Waters was admitted on a hospital hold for symptoms related to schizophrenia vs schizoaffective disorder. He was admitted on close status. At no time did Mr. Waters require seclusion and restraint for safety issues or gross behavioral dyscontrol. He required emergent medications for aggression/agitation twice but was willing to accept PO medications over IM at those times. On 9/14/2015 he was court committed and continued to refuse scheduled medication. At this time an ethics consult was placed and a request for a second physician opinion as well. On 09/21/2015, treatment team, a second opinion physician, and the ethics consult service decided to compel medication in this case. This was approved by the office of the Chief of Staff as well.

Mr. Waters presented with symptoms of schizoaffective including the following-paranoid and grandiose delusions, pressured speech, impulsivity, perseverative thought process, flight of ideas, distractability, and overvaluation of ideas. We started to address these symptoms by offering medications which he refused. After his court commitment and ethics consultation we started olanzapine based off the admission notes documentation of his mother stating it worked well for him in the past. On 09/29/2015, his mother called back and said the opposite, that he had a poor reaction with olanzapine in the past. At this time the treatment team decided to cross-taper Mr. Waters from olanzapine to aripiprazole. He requested some information on this new medication but agreed with treatment team to begin a trial. By 10/1, veteran was completely off olanzapine and on monotherapy aripiprazole. Dosage was titrated up to 15mg with appreciable side effects, and Mr. Waters' symptoms decreased substantially. On 10/14 his court commitment was dropped.

We also attempted engaged Mr. Waters in group and milieu activities. He said "I don't do groups," but he agreed to work individually with the recreational therapist during his time at the VA. Mr. Waters responded to these intervention with increased self-soothing behaviors, a greater ability to cope with others in the milieu.

Mr. Waters presented with no acute medial complaints and no chronic medical conditions requiring management while inpatient. He did complain of dry skin on his feet and was agreeable to topical treatments for this; he also had L shoulder pain that resolved with topical balms, and L jaw pain thought to be

---

secondary to clenching his teeth that resolved spontanously after 2 days of
symptomatic treatment with tylenol.

At time of discharge, Mr. Waters MSE was as follows:
Appearance: Well groomed, recently shaven man appearing stated age.
Behavior: No involuntary movements, shifts position occasion
fidget. Makes appropriate eye contact, frequently smiles.
Speech: Normal rate/tone/prosody/fluency/amount.
Mood: "I'm doing great"
Affect: Happy, congruent, non-restricted, not grandiose
Thought Process: Linear, goal-directed, logical
Thought Content: Focusing on details of discharge; getting m
collecting personal belongings, relaxing before friend comes to pick him up
Insight: Good - happy to have symptoms under control, sees medication playing
role in that
Judgment: Good - appropriately planning and advocating for himself
Cognition: Appropriate to situation, not formally assessed

Concern for imminent risk of suicide is deemed to be low .However, the immediate
risk is neither indicative nor predictive of future risks.This patient
does have some concerning risk factors for suicide, including
that he is male, single status,has a mental health diagnosis, has a history of
psychotic symptoms, and reported relationship problems with a partner in Mexico.

Mitigating factors for suicide risk include his current lack of psychotic
symptoms, lack of access to weapons, lack of alcohol or drug use,
lack of current SI and no history of previous SA/SIB,
positive social supports, protective religious/spiritual beliefs, sense of
responsibility to family and friends, and evidence of future-oriented thinking,
including planning how to get more of his medications once he leaves the
hospital, and plans to help take care of his mother's health condition after
discharge.

Modifiable risk factors were addressed during hospitalization through initiation
of appropriate pharmacotherapy, establishment of outpatient follow-up treatment,
and discussion with family.

FUNCTIONAL STATUS:
Return to normal activities as tolerated.

DISCHARGE MEDICATIONS:
Discharge Medication List (as given to patient):

These are your NEW medications:
1. AMMONIUM LACTATE 12% LOTION
     Apply sparingly topically to affected area twice a day as needed
     For dry skin on bilateral foot/heel
2. ARIPIPRAZOLE 30MG TAB
     Take one-half tablet by mouth at noon for psychosis

PATIENT NAME AND ADDRESS (Mechanical Imprinting, if available) | VISTA Electronic Medical Documentation

WATERS,TYRONE W
6805 NE BROADWAY
PORTLAND, OREGON 97213

Printed at PORTLAND VA MEDICAL CENTER

3. HYDROPHILIC (EQV AQUAPHOR) TOP OINT
     Apply thin film topically to affected area every day as needed
     For dry skin on bilateral feet

CLINICAL ISSUES REQUIRING FOLLOW UP DURING PC PHONE APT:
1. Able to continue taking medication as planned?
2. NEEDS PCP ASSIGNMENT AND FOLLOW UP
3.

ADDITIONAL FOLLOW UP APPOINTMENTS:
SPECIALTY   EXPECTED DATE   SCHEDULED(Y/N)   POINT OF
1. Dental consult   10/22   Portland, OR   Y
2. MHD with Dr. Brandon Cornejo, within 1 week   not yet scheduled
3. PCP to establish care; will be staying in Portland/Vancouver area and likely
transitioning to San Diego.

FOLLOW UP LABS INCLUDING PATHOLOGY & MICROBIOLOGY:
Screening labs for initiation of antipsychotics are ordered including HgbA1C,
fasting lipid profile, and an EKG

FOLLOW UP IMAGING AND PROCEDURES:
None

        MONITORING PROTOCOL FOR PATIENTS ON SECOND-GENERATION ANTIPSYCHOTICS**:

Obtain at baseline:
     No personal history of DM
     Weight (BMI): 145.3lb (BMI 22.8)
     Blood pressure: 115/77
   LIPIDS, FASTING   10/06/2015 15:00
     CHOLESTEROL   145
     TRIGLYCERIDES   188 H
     HDL CHOLESTER   53
     LDL-CHOL CALC   54
   GLUCOSE   72   10/06/2015 15:00
     HBA1C   5.4 4/2013

Obtain at 4 weeks:
     Weight (BMI)

Obtain at 8 weeks:
     Weight (BMI)

Obtain at 12 weeks:
     Weight (BMI)
     Blood pressure
     Fasting plasma glucose

PATIENT NAME AND ADDRESS (Mechanical Imprinting, if available) | VISTA Electronic Medical Documentation
WATERS, TYRONE W
6805 NE BROADWAY
PORTLAND, OREGON 97213

Printed at PORTLAND VA MEDICAL CENTER

Fasting lipid profile

Obtain quarterly:
     Weight (BMI)

Obtain annually:
     Personal/family history
     Waist circumference
     Blood pressure
     Fasting plasma glucose

Obtain every 5 years:
     Fasting lipid profile

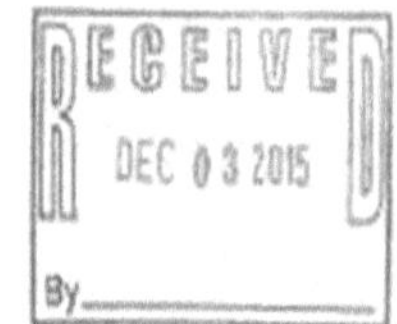

*More frequent assessments may be warranted based on clinical status.

**Consensus Development Conference on Antipsychotic Drugs and Obesity and Diabetes, 2004, Diabetes Care vol. 27 num. 2 pp. 596-601,
American Diabetes Association
American Psychiatric Association
American Association of Clinical Endocrinologists
North American Association for the Study of Obesity

/es/ EMILY T DEMARCO, MD
Psychiatry Resident
Signed: 10/16/2015 12:50

/es/ ...Brandon J. Cornejo MD, PhD
Psychiatrist
Cosigned: 10/16/2015 16:28

10/15/2015 ADDENDUM   STATUS: COMPLETED
Appointment with Cornejo 10/26/15 at 11:30AM

/es/ ...Brandon J. Cornejo MD, PhD
Psychiatrist
Signed: 10/16/2015 16:28

PATIENT NAME AND ADDRESS (Mechanical Imprinting, if available) | VISTA Electronic Medical Documentation
WATERS, TYRONE W
6805 NE BROADWAY
PORTLAND, OREGON 97213

Printed at PORTLAND VA MEDICAL CENTER

Death threat to Gov. Kate Brown shouldn't have spurred man's commitment, court rules

Updated May 9;
Posted May 9

Gov. Kate Brown received a death threat on her office's voicemail in June 2015. (Stephanie Yao Long/The Oregonian/File photo)

Waters, who was 49 then, is the son of former state Sen. Avel Gordly, who has spoken publicly of his struggles. Her advocacy for all people with mental illness prompted Oregon Health & Science University in 2008 to rename its behavioral health unit the Avel Gordly Center for Healing.

Neither Waters or Gordly could be reached for comment.

Waters' battles with mental illness began in his 20s, when he was diagnosed with schizophrenia. In 2001, he was sent to a Portland psychiatric hospital after he hallucinated and pointed a pellet gun at police officers in front of his grandfather's home in North Portland, according to the Appeals Court summary.

Waters stabilized on medication and did well for years after that, the court stated. He worked as a peer counselor for Cascadia Behavioral Health, but then switched medication and became consumed with fear about living in the United State as a gay, African American man, the court summary said.

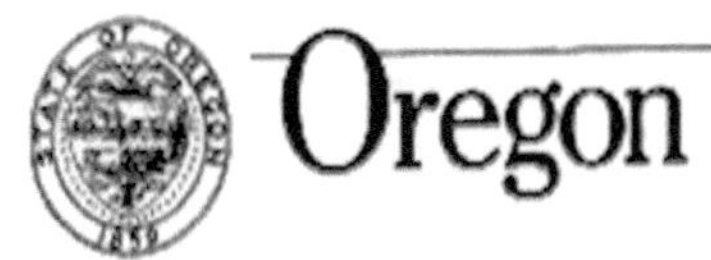

Office of Public Defense Services
1175 Court Street NE
Salem, Oregon 97301-4030
Telephone (503) 378-3349
Fax (503) 378-4462
www.oregon.gov/opds

May 17, 2018

Dear Mr. Waters,

Enclosed is the legal opinion from the Oregon Court of Appeals reversing your order of civil commitment. The State has 35 days to decide whether to appeal this decision to the Oregon Supreme Court. If they do not appeal the decision, the case will become finalized, and an appellate judgment will be created. My old office, Multnomah Defenders, retains your case and file, and continues to serve as your counsel. You can contact Joseph Debin at 503-226-3083 if you have additional questions regarding your case.

Sincerely,

Eric J. Deitrick
Deputy General Counsel
Office of Public Defense Services

IN THE COURT OF APPEALS OF THE
STATE OF OREGON

In the Matter of T. W.,
Alleged to be a Person with Mental Illness.
STATE OF OREGON,
Respondent,

v.

T. W.,
Appellant.

Multnomah County Circuit Court
15CC05146; A160465

Elizabeth Fithian-Barrett, Judge pro tempore.

Submitted May 17, 2016.

Eric J. Deitrick and Multnomah Defenders, Inc., filed the brief for appellant.

Ellen F. Rosenblum, Attorney General, Paul L. Smith, Deputy Solicitor General, and Susan Yorke, Assistant Attorney General, filed the brief for respondent.

Before DeVore, Presiding Judge, and Lagesen, Judge, and DeHoog, Judge.

DEHOOG, J.

Reversed.

Lagesen, J., dissenting.

hearing that is the subject of this case. His behavior shifted around the time that he was assigned a new counselor through the Department of Veterans' Affairs (VA) and he was prescribed a different medication that was not effective. He appeared to have relapsed—he experienced auditory hallucinations and struggled with behavioral issues, and his memory changed, causing him to believe that he was still in the 1990s. At some point after the period of stability, appellant was involved in an incident at the credit union office where he banked, resulting in him being barred from that office location.

In the fall of 2014, appellant left the Portland area; he spent some time in Seattle and then travelled to Canada with the intent of seeking "political asylum." He feared living in the United States as a gay black man with mental illness. In April 2015, after his request for asylum in Canada was denied, the Canadian authorities took him to the border, where he crossed into the State of Washington. He then spent time in Mexico and San Diego, California.

While appellant was in the San Diego area, he placed a call to Governor Brown's constituent office and left the following voicemail:

> "This message is for Governor Kate Brown. This is [appellant], the son of [a] former [state legislator]. Today is Monday, June 15th. Governor Brown, call off your wolves! Capiche? That means call off all of your fucking agents, actors, and whatever the fuck else your goddam problem is, bitch! You'll die! I consider you, bitch, a fucking enemy. * * * I'll kill you! Do you fucking understand? I'll fucking kill you, bitch! You're an enemy. * * * Don't fuck with me, I'll kill you dead, bitch! You're a dead fucking bitch! Three times! This time I'll walk up, and this fucking day you are dead bitch! Fucking dead! * * * You're dead! * * *."

Oregon State Police Officer Schinnerer, who was on assignment with the Governor's protection unit, was very concerned by the voicemail. According to Schinnerer, although hostile phone calls to the Governor's office are not uncommon, appellant's voicemail was of a different intensity than other calls. As a result, he began to investigate and attempted to locate appellant. Schinnerer contacted appellant's mother and learned that appellant was in the San throughout his trip from California and that he had taken a video of the individuals with his cell phone, though not while they were harassing him. Appellant permitted Burley to view the video; Burley testified that it appeared to him as though the passengers in the video were unaware that they were being video recorded and that they had no interest in appellant whatsoever—they were simply sitting and reading books or newspapers.

Appellant told Burley that he was a volunteer security person for Amtrak—that he had been asked to provide security while riding the train. He also stated that he was a volunteer bounty hunter and helped out bounty hunter agencies. In that capacity, according to appellant, he followed people, gathered intelligence on them, and provided bounty hunters with information about people he perceived to have broken the law. Appellant also told Burley that, if he saw something suspicious, he would let law enforcement know something was going on. Burley asked appellant whether he would take a person into custody and take law enforcement action if he believed that the person was a criminal. Appellant did not answer that question. Hackett told Burley that she wanted to place a hold on appellant, and the group of responders created a plan to have appellant transported to the hospital; he was later admitted to the VA hospital and housed in the inpatient psychiatric unit pending his hearing.

The trial court held a commitment hearing on September 14, 2015, and appellant testified. He stated that he did not believe that he needed medication and that, when he used ear plugs, he did not hear voices. He also stated that he felt uncomfortable staying in Oregon and wanted to live somewhere other than the United States because of how he had been treated. He denied having done anything to protect himself when harassed other than to call law enforcement to have them address the situation. He explained that, although he had purchased mace, he had not used it on anyone, and, although he had a flashlight, he had not beaten anyone with it. He denied buying or owning any firearms. He further testified that he did not want to hurt himself or hurt or kill anyone else, including the Governor or other state officials.

and a danger to himself, and is unlikely and unwilling to participate in voluntary treatments." *See* ORS 426.130; ORS 426.005(1)(f)(A). On appeal, appellant does not dispute that he has a mental disorder. Rather, he contends that the record lacks clear and convincing evidence that he was a danger to himself or others at the time of the hearing. In response, the state asserts that sufficient evidence supports the trial court's determination that appellant posed a danger to others.

"The clear and convincing evidence standard is a rigorous one, requiring evidence that is of extraordinary persuasiveness, and which makes the fact in issue highly probable." *State v. M. R.*, 225 Or App 569, 574, 202 P3d 221 (2009) (internal quotation marks omitted). To prove that a person is a danger to himself, the state must show that his "mental disorder will cause him to behave in a way that is likely to result in *actual serious physical harm* to himself in the near future." *State v. L. D.*, 247 Or App 394, 399, 270 P3d 324 (2011) (emphasis in original). We have previously concluded that "a person can be deemed dangerous to self if he *** has established a pattern in the past of taking certain actions that lead to self-destructive conduct, and then he *** begins to follow the pattern again." *State v. Roberts*, 183 Or App 520, 524, 52 P3d 1123 (2002). However, "the required expectation of actual serious physical harm must be established by more than mere speculation or conjecture." *L. D.*, 247 Or App at 399.

In addition, we have explained that "delusional or eccentric behavior—even behavior that may be inherently risky—is not necessarily sufficient to warrant commitment." *State v. Olsen*, 208 Or App 686, 691, 145 P3d 350 (2006); *see also Roberts*, 183 Or App at 525 (although the appellant frequently wandered the streets in a confused state of mind, there was no evidence that that activity had led to physical injury). Further, the "abstract possibility that a person's bizarre and agitated behavior might theoretically draw a violent response from someone cannot satisfy the requirement that the threat of harm be real, rather than speculative, and exist in the near future." *State v. J. G.*, 218 Or App 398, 401, 180 P3d 63, *rev den*, 345 Or 94 (2008) (internal insufficient to support the trial court's determination that appellant is a danger to himself.[4]

We turn, then, to the second basis for appellant's commitment. To prove that a person is a danger to others, the state "generally must offer more than evidence of appellant's threats of future violence, such as a corresponding overt act demonstrating an intention to carry out the threats or other circumstances indicating that actual future violence is highly likely." *L. D.*, 247 Or App at 400. "Mere verbal threats of violence are generally insufficient to establish danger to others." *State v. E. D.*, 264 Or App 71, 74, 331 P3d 1032 (2014) "However, if a mentally ill person has threatened others and has also carried out an overt violent act in the past against another person, those facts generally constitute clear and convincing evidence that the person is a danger to others." *State v. D. L. W.*, 244 Or App 401, 405, 260 P3d 691 (2011); *cf. E. D.*, 264 Or App at 75 (the appellant did not present a danger to himself or others when he committed only "one overt violent act—initiating [a] fistfight—and [made] a few vague threats of violence"). "Whether a person is a danger to others is determined by his condition at the time of the hearing as understood in the context of his history." *E. D.*, 264 Or App at 74 (internal quotation marks and brackets omitted).

On appeal, the state argues that appellant's recent verbal acts and his behavioral history provide a foundation for predicting his future dangerousness. The state points to appellant's threatening voicemail to Governor Brown, which understandably was taken seriously by investigators. That threat, the state argues, along with appellant's fixation on his perceived persecution by others, his use of profanities toward strangers, his delusional belief that he is a bounty hunter, his decision to arm himself with pepper spray, handcuffs, and a large metal flashlight, and his prior altercation with the police, collectively support a finding that appellant

---

[4] The dissent takes issue with our description of the use of beanbag rounds to subdue appellant as a "precaution." We do not mean to suggest that such measures are not serious or that they do not carry a significant risk of harm. We merely observe that, notwithstanding that fact, that incident says little if anything about whether appellant presented a risk to himself or others at the time of the hearing.

sufficient to support finding of danger to others when the appellant made threats to blow up mayor's house and office without any evidence he committed an overt act to follow up on the threats).

Notwithstanding the absence of overt acts of violence in appellant's history, the state urges us to conclude that appellant's current delusional behavior, viewed in light of his history, is sufficient support for the trial court's determination that appellant is a danger to others; we disagree, however, that those circumstances can support the determination that actual future violence is highly likely. We note that, even though appellant believes himself to be a volunteer bounty hunter, there is no evidence in the record indicating that he ever acted in furtherance of that belief in a manner that involved or that might have resulted in violence on appellant's part. For example, there is no evidence that he has ever attempted to make an arrest, take anyone into custody, or otherwise act out on his belief that he is a bounty hunter in a violent manner. It is true that he wore a security guard uniform on the train, carried handcuffs and a Maglite capable of being used as a weapon, and possessed pepper spray; there was no evidence, however, that he had ever used those items against anyone. Further, the record indicates that appellant's plan was to report information of wrongdoing to bounty hunters or law enforcement. And, even when appellant experienced delusions that a woman on the Portland-bound train wanted to harm him, he did not act out physically. Instead, he called her a profane name and recorded a video with his phone. Notably, appellant ultimately cooperated with the conductor's request by moving to a different location on the train, after which, according to his own testimony, appellant called the FBI to seek assistance with the people who wanted to harm him. Nothing about those circumstances reflect an individual who is likely to act out violently as a result of his mental disorder.

Finally, the state relies on appellant's prior encounter with the police as evidence supporting the trial court's determination that appellant is a danger to others. We recognize that appellant's mother testified that his current symptoms were similar to, but more intense than, those that he exhibited at the time of the police encounter. However,

At the time of the hearing, appellant was suffering from a very specific delusion as a result of his mental disorder: He was a private security professional who provided security services for Amtrak and assisted bounty hunters. Appellant was not merely suffering from the delusion, he was acting in accordance with it. He had a uniform. He had a duty belt. He was equipped with some of the tools of the trade: handcuffs, a flashlight of the type that law enforcement is trained to use as a "striking instrument," and pepper spray.[1] Appellant also believed that several people, if not more, were after him and wanted him dead.

The psychiatrist who examined appellant opined that appellant's delusion "would put him in harm's way" and pose a risk of harm to others, due to the particular nature of the profession of which appellant believed he was a part: "[T]hat's a violent profession, or can be a violent profession, and with his grandiose and paranoid delusions I think that there is a reasonable probability that there could be some violence involved." One of the police officers involved in taking appellant in for a mental health evaluation elaborated on the nature of the risk that appellant faced if he acted in accordance with his delusion: "[H]e'd definitely be putting himself in harm's way attempting to take somebody into custody or taking law enforcement action when he's not a—a trained person."

Appellant's delusions previously have put him at risk of harm. In 2001, they led to an incident in which he pulled out a pellet gun when confronted by police. This, in turn, led to police firing at appellant with beanbag rounds.[2]

---

[1] At the time that appellant was taken in for evaluation, the pepper spray was in appellant's baggage and not in its holster on appellant's duty belt. It is not unreasonable to think that appellant had stowed it in his baggage for purposes of the train trip and would have put it in its holster in the near future.

[2] The majority opinion characterizes the use of beanbag rounds as a "precaution." I see nothing in the record that permits the inference that the rounds were precautionary, as distinct from a preliminary effort to subdue appellant using nonlethal force before resorting to lethal force. Regardless, the fact that beanbag rounds are nonlethal does not mean that appellant was not at risk of physical harm in the prior incident. The Ninth Circuit has explained the operation of beanbag rounds:

"The shot is not like a regular bullet—it does not normally rip through soft tissue and bone on contact with the human body. It is designed to knock down a target, rendering the individual incapable of resistance, without

I recognize that appellant's delusion had not yet resulted in physical harm to anyone, and that it is not certain that it would. But certainty that a person is dangerous, or even proof beyond a reasonable doubt that a person is dangerous, is not required for civil commitments in Oregon. The point of the civil commitment statutes is to ensure that persons whose mental disorders make them "likely to be dangerous" receive needed treatment, averting the risk that a person's mental disorder will lead to serious harm or death. *See Addington v. Texas*, 441 US 418, 428-29, 99 S Ct 1804, 60 L Ed 2d 323 (1979) (discussing the interests animating civil commitment statutes). As we have explained, "grave physical harm need not actually occur before a court may find a person to be mentally ill who is dangerous to him or herself or others." *State v. C. C.*, 258 Or App 727, 735, 311 P3d 948 (2013). Rather, it simply must be inferable that, given the particular facts of a case, such harm is highly likely to occur in the near future if the person's mental disorder is not treated. *See id.* In my view, that inference permissibly can be drawn from the specific facts present in this case.

TYRONE WATERS PROTESTING AT A PEACE RALLY
PEACEFULLYAGAINST POLICE BRUTALITY AND ASKING
FOR POLICE ACCOUNTABILITY IN PORTLAND, OREGON
AND NATIONWIDE.

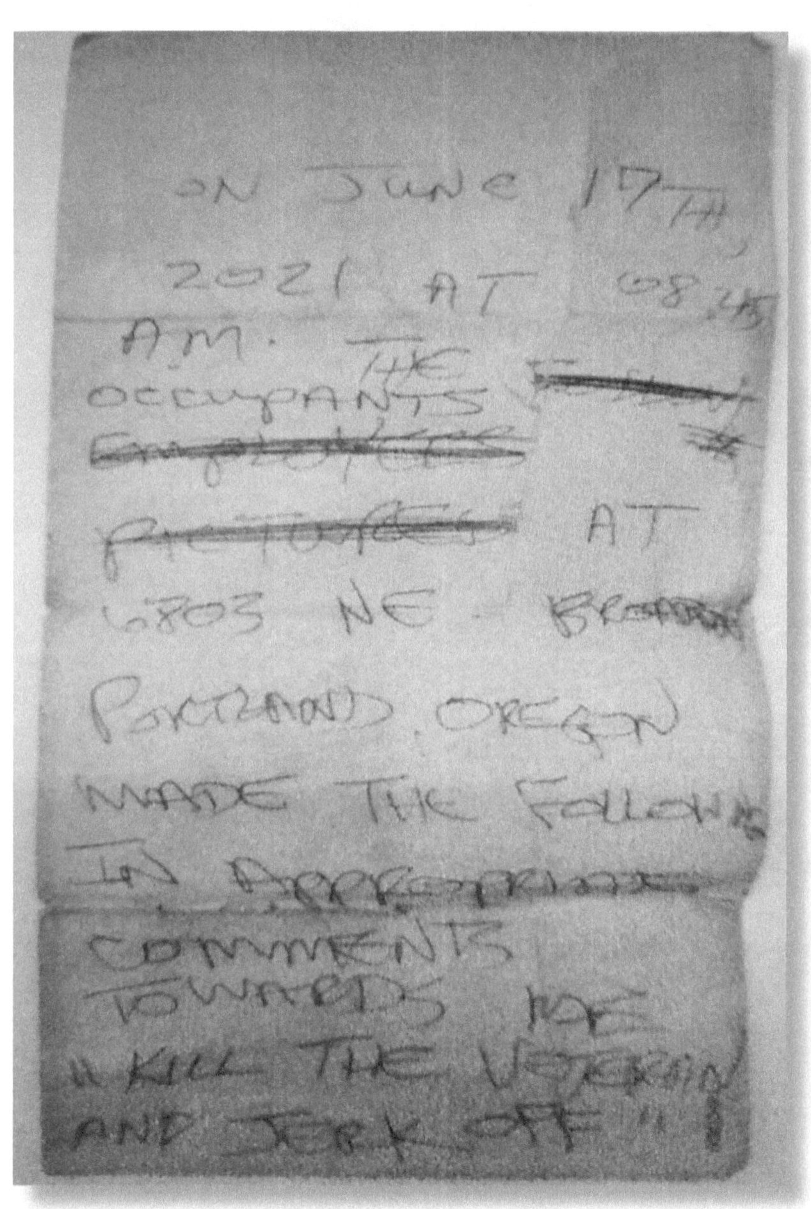

ON JUNE 17TH,
2021 AT 08:45
A.M. THE
OCCUPANTS
AT
6803 NE
PORTLAND, OREGON
MADE THE FOLLOWING
IN APPROPRIATE
COMMENTS
TOWARDS ME
"KILL THE VETERAN
AND JERK OFF!!!"

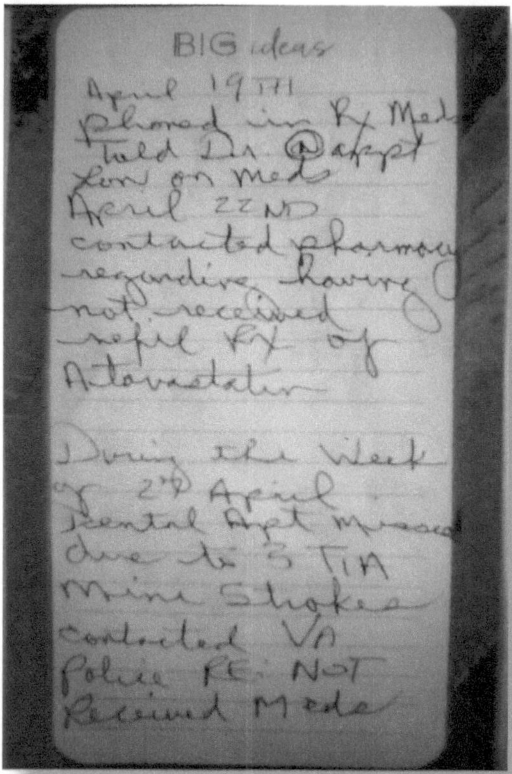

BIG ideas

April 19TH
Phoned in Rx Meds
Told Dr. @ appt
low on meds
April 22ND
contacted pharmacy
regarding having
not received
refil Rx of
Atorvastatin

During the Week
of 2ND April
Dental Apt Missed
due to 5 TIA
Mini Strokes
Contacted VA
Police RE: NOT
Received Meds

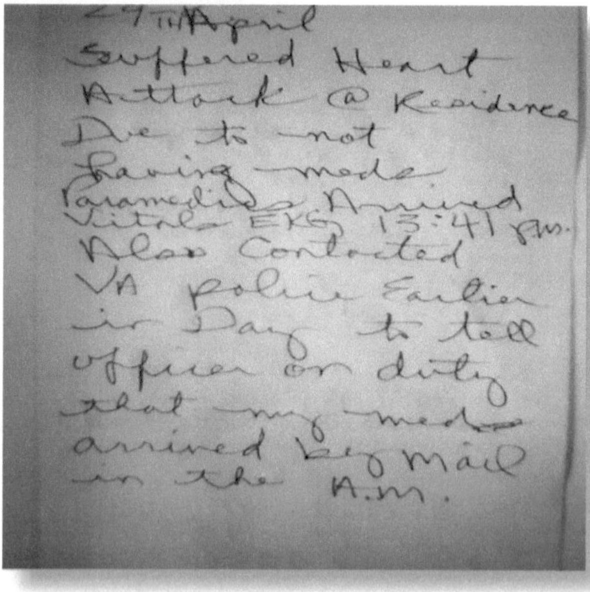

29TH April
Suffered Heart
Attack @ Residence
Due to not
having meds.
Paramedics Arrived
Vitals EKG 13:41 P.M.
Also Contacted
VA Police Earlier
in Day to tell
officer on duty
that my meds
arrived by mail
in the
A.M.

My white supremacist neighbors at 6809 NE Broadway in Portland OR blocked me with her car so that I could not access my ford crown victoria police interceptor

I went shopping at QFC and someone put fecal matter on my shopping cart while I was shopping in Portland OR

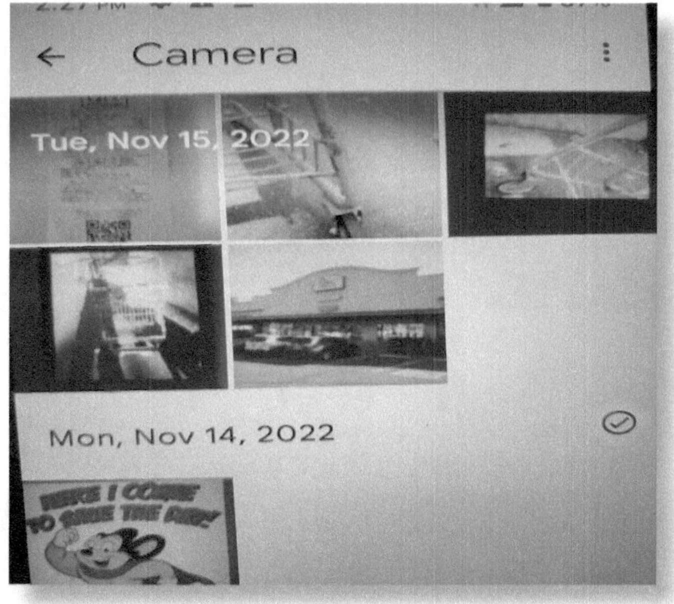

Know the signs
of stroke and
act FAST
In stroke, every second counts.
Quick action can limit damage
and help lead to a full recovery.
Use "FAST" to remember the signs
of stroke and to act quickly:
Facial weakness — Can the
person smile? Has their mouth or
eye drooped?
Arm weakness — Can the person
hold up both arms equally?
Speech problems — Can the
person speak clearly and understand what you say?
Time to call 911 — If even one of
these problems is new.
If you feel these signs, call 911. Do
not drive yourself to the hospital.
Brought to you by the National
Stroke Association and Legacy
Health's nationally certified stroke
program.
Our legacy is yours.

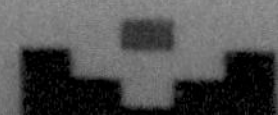

Emergency Medical Service (EMS) Discharge from Scene
Date
Incident Location
Patient Name
Agency Run Number

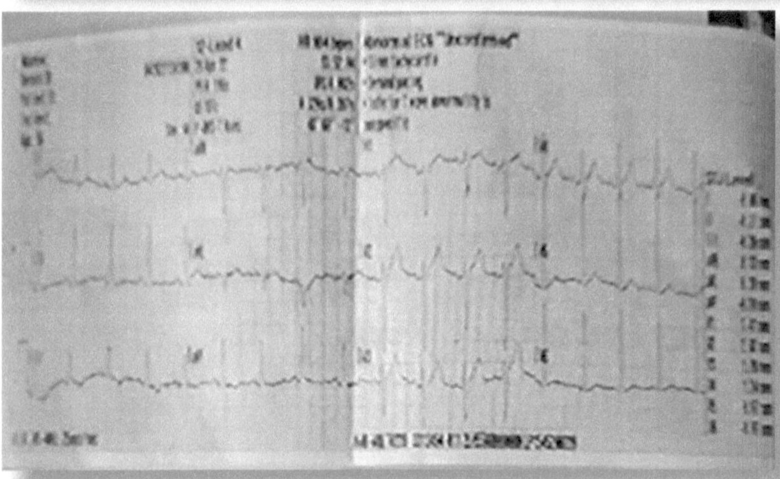

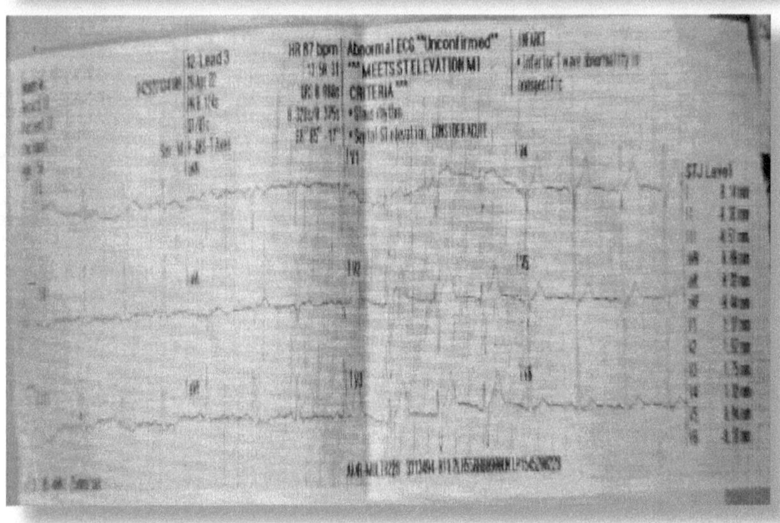

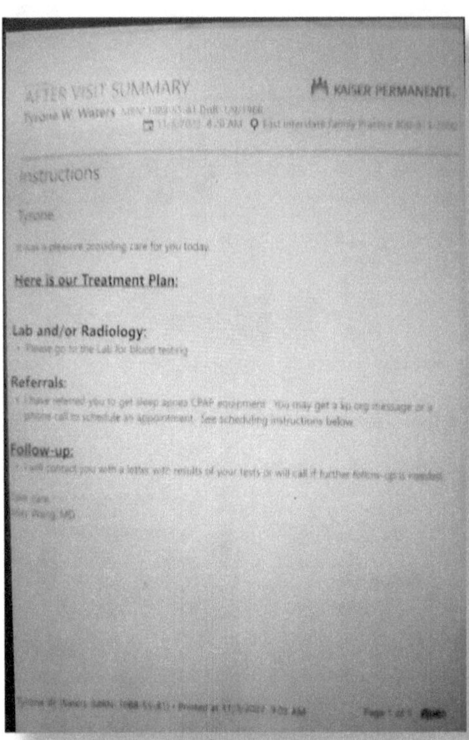

AFTER VISIT SUMMARY

Tysone W. Waters   KAISER PERMANENTE.

11/3/2022 4:30 AM   East Interstate Family Practice

Instructions

Tysone

It was a pleasure providing care for you today.

Here is our Treatment Plan:

Lab and/or Radiology:
- Please go to the Lab for blood testing

Referrals:
- I have referred you to get sleep apnea CPAP equipment. You may get a kp.org message or a phone call to schedule an appointment. See scheduling instructions below.

Follow-up:
- I will contact you with a letter with results of your tests or will call if further follow-up is needed.

May Pang, MD

Tysone W. Waters (MRN: 1088-55-81) • Printed at 11/3/2022 9:03 AM   Page 1 of 3

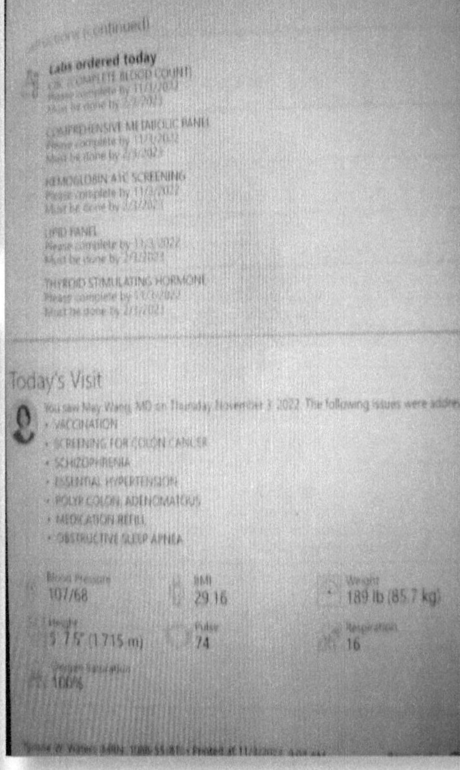

...more (continued)

Labs ordered today

CBC (COMPLETE BLOOD COUNT)
Please complete by 11/3/2022
Must be done by 2/3/2023

COMPREHENSIVE METABOLIC PANEL
Please complete by 11/3/2022
Must be done by 2/3/2023

HEMOGLOBIN A1C SCREENING
Please complete by 11/3/2022
Must be done by 2/3/2023

LIPID PANEL
Please complete by 11/3/2022
Must be done by 2/3/2023

THYROID STIMULATING HORMONE
Please complete by 11/3/2022
Must be done by 2/3/2023

Today's Visit

You saw May Wang, MD on Thursday, November 3, 2022. The following issues were addressed:
- VACCINATION
- SCREENING FOR COLON CANCER
- SCHIZOPHRENIA
- ESSENTIAL HYPERTENSION
- POLYP COLON, ADENOMATOUS
- MEDICATION REFILL
- OBSTRUCTIVE SLEEP APNEA

Blood Pressure 107/68

BMI 29.16

Weight 189 lb (85.7 kg)

Height 5' 7.5" (1.715 m)

Pulse 74

Respiration 16

Oxygen Saturation 100%

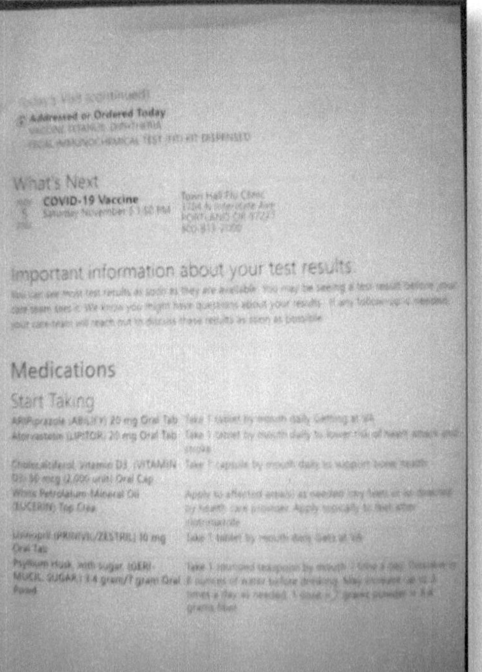

Today's Visit (continued)

Addressed or Ordered Today
VACCINE, TETANUS, DIPHTHERIA
FECAL IMMUNOCHEMICAL TEST (FIT) KIT DISPENSED

What's Next

COVID-19 Vaccine
Saturday November 5 3:00 PM

Town Hall Flu Clinic
3704 N Interstate Ave
PORTLAND OR 97227
800-813-2000

Important information about your test results

You can see most test results as soon as they are available. You may be seeing a test result before your care team sees it. We know you might have questions about your results. If any follow-up is needed, your care team will reach out to discuss these results as soon as possible.

Medications

Start Taking

ARIPiprazole (ABILIFY) 20 mg Oral Tab — Take 1 tablet by mouth daily. Getting at VA

Atorvastatin (LIPITOR) 20 mg Oral Tab — Take 1 tablet by mouth daily to lower risk of heart attack and stroke

Cholecalciferol, Vitamin D3 (VITAMIN D3) 50 mcg (2,000 unit) Oral Cap — Take 1 capsule by mouth daily to support bone health

White Petrolatum-Mineral Oil (EUCERIN) Top Crea — Apply to affected area(s) as needed (dry feet) or as directed by health care provider. Apply topically to feet after moisturizing.

Lisinopril (PRINIVIL/ZESTRIL) 10 mg Oral Tab — Take 1 tablet by mouth daily. Gets at VA

Psyllium Husk, with sugar (GERI-MUCIL SUGAR) 3.4 gram/7 gram Oral Powd — Take 1 rounded teaspoon by mouth 1 time a day. Dissolve in 8 ounces of water before drinking. May increase up to 3 times a day as needed. 1 dose = 2 grams powder = 3.4 grams fiber.

Tysone W. Waters (MRN: 1088-55-81) • Printed at 11/3/2022 9:03 AM   Page 3 of 3

ON 3 NOVEMBER 2022 I HAD
A ROUTINE PHYSICAL AT KAISER
PERMANENTE AND GIVEN A
REFERRAL TO GET SLEEP APNEA
CPAP EQUIPMENT FOR CHRONIC
SLEEP APNEA
ON 22 NOVEMBER 2022 AT 08:45
ANDREW FROM THE KAISER SLEEP
CLINIC CALLED TO CANCEL MY
APPOINTMENT AND STATED NO
PROVIDER AVAILABLE ON TODAY

ON 6 DECEMBER 2022 AT 14:45 PM
I HAD AN APPOINTMENT WITH
THE KAISER SLEEP CLINIC
WITH HOLLY WHO TOLD ME
SHE WOULD PUT IN A REFERRAL
TO APRIA FOR ME TO GET

A CPAP MACHINE
HOLLY FURTHER STATED
TO CALL APRIA ON FRIDAY
OR MONDAY

ON 12 DECEMBER 2022 I
CALLED APRIA TO CONFIRM
RECEIPT OF A REFERRAL
FROM KAISER PERMANENTE
FOR MY CPAP MACHINE
I WAS TOLD THERE WAS
NO RECORD OF A REFERRAL
AND NO ORDER FOR A
CPAP MACHINE I THEN
CALLED KAISER PERMANENTE
TO REPORT THIS THEY TOLD
ME THEY HAD NO RECORD

TO CALL BACK TO
KAISER PERMANENTE
AND REQUEST ANOTHER
DOCTOR. I THEN
SPOKE TO ALLEN ON
THE SUPERVISORY LEADERSHIP
TEAM AT KAISER PERMANENTE
WHO THEN CHANGED MY
PRIMARY CARE DOCTOR
OF RECORD

TO THIS DATE I STILL
HAVE NOT RECEIVED A
CPAP MACHINE FOR MY
CHRONIC CONDITION

I ALSO TRIED TO REPORT
THIS INCIDENT TO PORTLAND
POLICE NON-EMERGENCY AND
THE OPERATOR HUNG UP ON ME

OF THE APPOINTMENT AND
NO RECORD OF A CPAP
MACHINE BEING ORDERED
AS STATED BY A MEMBER
OF THE KAISER PERMANENTE
LEADERSHIP TEAM

I THEN STATED TO THAT
PERSON THAT THIS IS
PATIENT ABUSE ASSAULT
AND BATTERY CONSPIRACY
TO COMMIT MURDER AND
THAT I WOULD REPORT
THIS TO THE F.B.I.
AND DID SO AFTER
TALKING TO A FEDERAL
AGENT OF THE FBI
HE INSTRUCTED ME

Our failed Portland City Leaders.

The New York Times
The Washington Post
MSNBC
CBS
abc
CNN
NBC

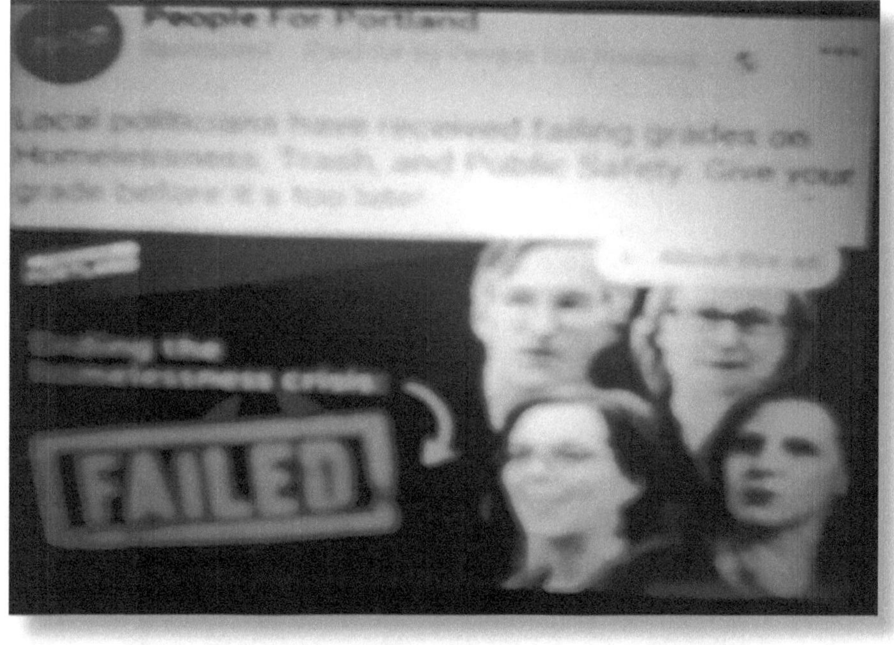

People For Portland
Local politicians have received failing grades on Homelessness, Trash, and Public Safety. Give your grade before it's too late!
FAILED!

While at medical appointment at kaiser permamente a vehicle with cancer causing bio hazard asbestos was parked next to our vehicle.

SPEAKER TINA KOTEK
HER WAY HAS ONLY MADE THINGS WORSE

SMEARS
FROM THE
THOUGHT POLICE

Tyrone, the 2022 US midterm elections are November 8!
Find where to return your ballot and other info about the 2022 US midterm elections. Share to encourage others to vote.

SILENT READING HOUR

THIS IS WHERE YOU FIND OUT WHO IS REALLY OPEN FOR YOU

Listening Meeting

We all have concerns about safety at the Binford and our surrounding areas.

NE Precinct Commander Erika Hurley and US Attorney Craig Gabriel are coming to listen to those concerns and to hear suggestions for addressing them.

Thursday, August 19 at 4:00 PM
Front yard of Building 3
Bring your own chair

This is the first time we've had a "Listening Meeting" with law enforcement.

If you have any questions - OR - If you can't attend, please submit your questions or ideas to binfordbd@gmail.com.

This is how many times the police were called out to my residence at
the Ellington Apartments and the Binford Condominuims

5/1/19   19:15 (P.M.

CITY OF PORTLAND, OREGON
Officer Michael Gonzalez #57145

CITY OF PORTLAND, OREGON
Officer Larry Wingfield

CITY OF PORTLAND, OREGON
Officer Greg Budey

CITY OF PORTLAND, OREGON
Officer Joshua Letter

CITY OF PORTLAND, OREGON
Officer Suciu

CITY OF PORTLAND, OREGON
Officer Randi Miller

CITY OF PORTLAND, OREGON
Officer Jim Ferner

CITY OF PORTLAND, OREGON
Officer Wendi Hamm

CITY OF PORTLAND, OREGON
Officer De Andre Amos

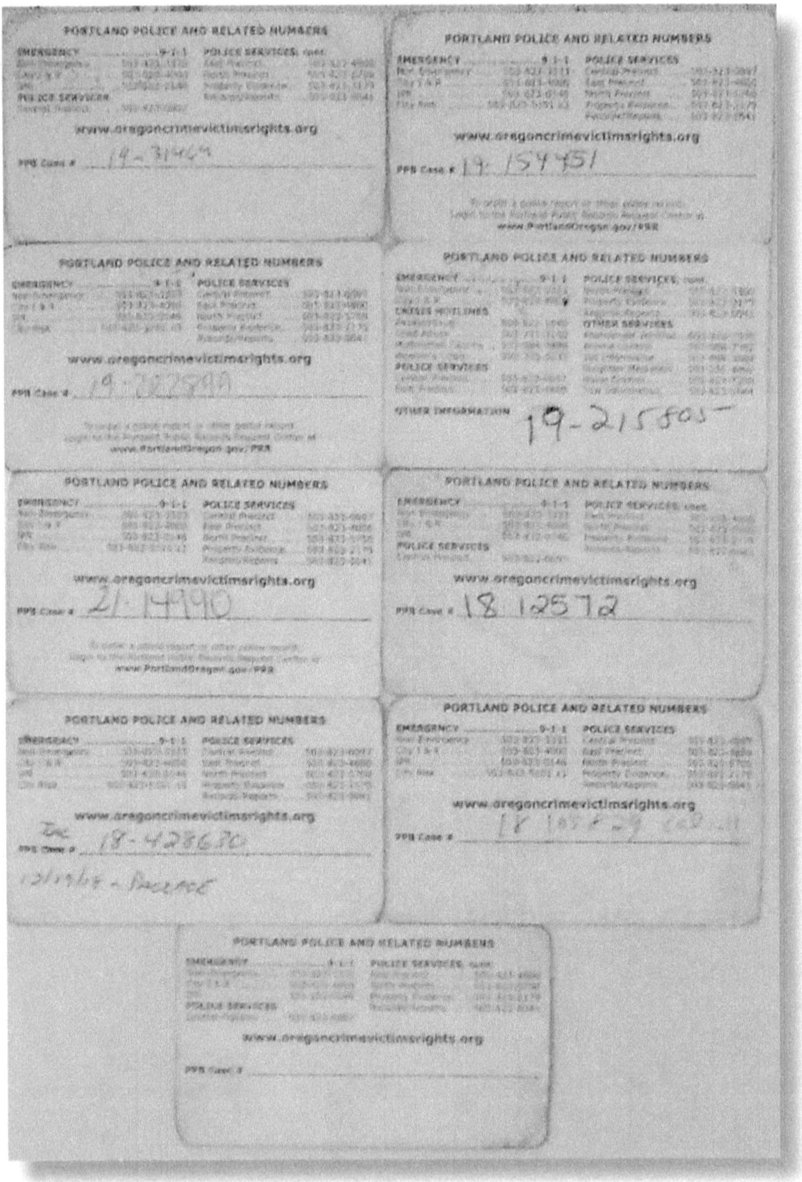

PORTLAND POLICE AND RELATED NUMBERS

www.oregoncrimevictimsrights.org

PPB Case # 19-31969

PORTLAND POLICE AND RELATED NUMBERS

www.oregoncrimevictimsrights.org

PPB Case # 19-154951

PORTLAND POLICE AND RELATED NUMBERS

www.oregoncrimevictimsrights.org

PPB Case # 19-302899A

PORTLAND POLICE AND RELATED NUMBERS

www.oregoncrimevictimsrights.org

OTHER INFORMATION 19-215805

PORTLAND POLICE AND RELATED NUMBERS

www.oregoncrimevictimsrights.org

PPB Case # 21-14790

PORTLAND POLICE AND RELATED NUMBERS

www.oregoncrimevictimsrights.org

PPB Case # 18-12572

PORTLAND POLICE AND RELATED NUMBERS

www.oregoncrimevictimsrights.org

PPB Case # 18-428670

PORTLAND POLICE AND RELATED NUMBERS

www.oregoncrimevictimsrights.org

PPB Case # 18-1057-9

PORTLAND POLICE AND RELATED NUMBERS

www.oregoncrimevictimsrights.org

PPB Case #

NAACP
THIS IS POWER
ALASKA OREGON WASHINGTON STATE AREA CONFERENCE
ANNUAL CONVENTION
September 2nd - 4th, 2022
PORTLAND, OREGON
VOTE!
This is Power
Justice for Breonna Taylor
JUSTICE 4 ARMAUD ARBERY
Our Voice is Our Power VOTE!
NAACP YOUTH

REV. DR. Tyrone Waters picture with civil rights
Attorney Ben Crump.

"Attorney Ben Crump"

NAVY

REV. DR. Tyrone Waters meal served at NAACP conference.

The following crime incident was reported to Portland Police. Our vechile was broken into during the early morning hours of January 5th, 2023 we are victims of a hate crime and fearful of threats to life and property see photo of vandalism to our vehicle.

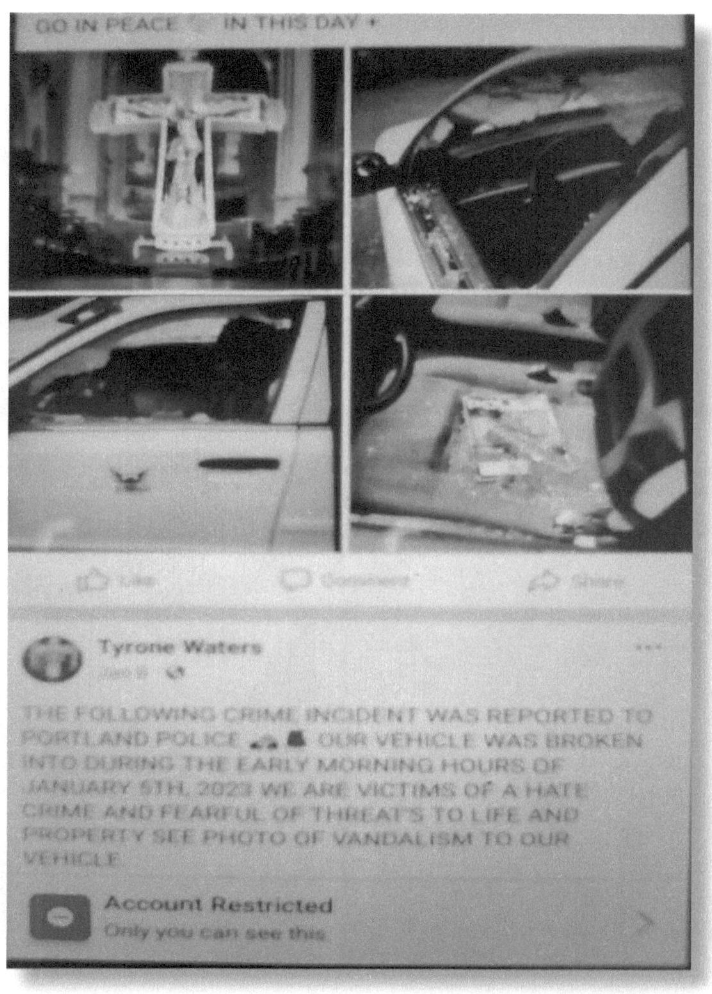

February 9th, 2023 at approximately 11:10am, this male attempted to break in to my residence in Portland Oregon

ON FEBRUARY 28TH, 2023 SHORTLY AFTER 1PM AT THE BINFORD CONDOMINIUMS IN PORTLAND, OREGON GARY THE LANDSCAPE PERSONEL TOLD ME I WAS DEAD CALLED ME A NIGGER AND SAID YOU LOSE. THIS ACTIVITY BEHAVIOR IS CONDONED BY BRIDGE CITY COMMUNITY MANAGEMENT PROPERTY MANAGER FOR THE BINFORD CONDOMINIUMS AND THIS IS ALSO THEIR GENETIC CORPORATE POSTURE.

STAY TUNED

BOYCOTT
DELTA AIRLINES
GATHER YOUR GROUP
JOIN THE CONVERSATION
TODAY & EVERY DAY

Thank you for reading my scandalous book. Please share this information with others. While traveling in flight, Take time to read my book.

Inside the weapons that may change your life

Despite breakthrouhghs this remains the number 1 killer

in the United States of American it's what works.

Here's why and what may help.

A book for through times.

Rebuke death in Jesus name.